A Journey Through Acts

The 50 Day Bible Challenge

A Journey
Through Acts

The 50 Day Bible Challenge

Edited by Marek P. Zabriskie

FORWARD MOVEMENT

Cincinnati, Ohio

To Emily, Marguerite, and Isabelle,
Thank you for inspiring me and many others with your lives.

Foreword

The stories and teachings of Jesus are dangerous! Not because they hurt and not because they bring harm, but the stories of Jesus are dangerous because they bear a Word not created or controlled by any person, interest group, party, or self-interest of this world.

These stories and teachings point to the deep wisdom embedded in the way of Jesus, which is nothing less than the way of the very love of God. And that way invariably turns the way we often are and the way the world often is upside-down—which is really right-side up. In this way, the stories and teachings of Jesus—and the witness of those who followed him—help, heal, lift up, and set the captive free.

The Acts of the Apostles tells of the earliest people who dared to follow the way of Jesus, actually living by what he taught, living in his Spirit, and walking his way, day by day.

The disciples were not paragons of perfection. They didn't always get it right. They were good and gracious, fallible, sinful, human—like the rest of us. But they followed Jesus. They became his movement in their time. And eventually, the world around them noticed a difference in them.

One story from Acts describes these earliest folk who dared to be disciples of this Jesus:

> These people who have been turning the world upside down have come here also…They are all acting contrary to the decrees of the emperor, saying that there is another king named Jesus.
>
> —Acts 17:6b-7

The stories and teachings of Jesus are dangerous because anyonewho takes them seriously enough to live like Jesus, to be a part of his movement in the world, may well be accused of turning the world upside down.

So I invite you to take the 50 Day Bible Challenge, to read and meditate on the Acts of the Apostles—and if you're so inspired, to read Acts' companion book, the Gospel of Luke. But more than that, I invite you, like those who were the Jesus Movement in the first century, to dare anew to live the Jesus way, day by day. And maybe it will be said of us, too: "These people are turning the world upside down!"

Your brother in Christ,

Michael B. Curry
Presiding Bishop of the Episcopal Church

How to Read the Bible Prayerfully

Welcome to The 50 Day Bible Challenge. We are delighted that you are interested in reading God's life-transforming Word from the Book of Acts. It will change and enrich your life. Here are some suggestions to consider as you get started:

- You can begin The 50 Day Bible Challenge at any time of year. It works especially well for the fifty days of Eastertide, beginning on Easter Day. It also could be read during Lent, beginning on the Sunday before Ash Wednesday.

- Each day has a manageable amount of reading, a meditation, questions for thought or discussion, and a prayer, written by a host of wonderful authors.

- We suggest that you try to read the Bible each day. This is a great spiritual discipline to establish.

- If you need more than fifty days to read through the Book of Acts, we support you in moving at the pace that works best for you.

- The full text of Acts is included in this book, but many Bible Challenge participants also enjoy reading the Bible on an iPad, iPhone, Kindle, or Nook or listening to the Bible on CDs or on a mobile device using Audio.com, faithcomesbyhearing.org, or Pandora radio. Find what works for you.

How to Read the Bible

Because the Bible is holy scripture, read it with a reverent spirit. We advocate a devotional approach to reading the Bible, rather than reading it as a purely intellectual or academic exercise.

- Before reading the Bible, take a moment of silence to put yourself in the presence of God. We then invite you to read this prayer written by Archbishop Thomas Cranmer.

   > Blessed Lord, who has caused all holy scriptures to be written for our learning: Grant us to hear them, read, mark, learn, and inwardly digest them, that we may embrace and ever hold fast the blessed hope of everlasting life, which you have given us in our Savior Jesus Christ; who lives and reigns with you and the Holy Spirit, one God, for ever and ever. *Amen.*

- Consider using the ancient monastic practice of *lectio divina*. In this form of Bible reading, you read the text and then meditate on a portion of it—be it a verse or two or even a single word. Mull over the words and their meaning. Then offer a prayer to God based on what you have read, how it has made you feel, or what it has caused you to ponder. Listen in silence for God to respond to your prayer.

- We encourage you to read in the morning, if possible, so that your prayerful reading may spiritually enliven the rest of your day. If you cannot read in the morning, read at a time that suits the rhythm of your life.

- Have fun and find spiritual peace and the joy that God desires for you in your daily reading.

Sharing The 50 Day Bible Challenge with Others

One way to hold yourself accountable to reading God's Word is to form a group within your church or community. By participating in The 50 Day Bible Challenge together, you can support one another in your reading, discuss the Bible passages, ask questions, and share how God's Word is transforming your life.

- Ask to have a notice printed in your church newsletter that you are starting a group to participate in The 50 Day Bible Challenge. Invite others to join you and to gather regularly to discuss the readings, ask questions, and share how it is transforming your life. Visit the Center for Biblical Studies website (www.thecenterforbiblicalstudies.org) to see more suggestions about how churches can participate in The Bible Challenge.

- If you form a Bible Challenge group, consider holding a gathering or meal to celebrate your spiritual accomplishment.

- If you do not want to join a group, you may wish to invite a friend or family member (or two) to share The 50 Day Bible Challenge with you.

- After participating in The 50 Day Bible Challenge, you will be more equipped to support and mentor others in reading the Bible.

- If you find reading the entire Bible and being part of The Bible Challenge to be a blessing in your life, then we strongly encourage you to share the blessing. Invite several friends or family members to participate in The Bible Challenge.

The Bible Challenge—Read the Bible in a Year

After completing the 50 Day Bible challenge, we encourage you to accept the challenge to read the entire Bible in a year. Reading the Bible each day is a great spiritual discipline to establish. The goal of the Center for Biblical Studies is to help you discover God's wisdom and to create a lifelong spiritual practice of daily Bible reading so that God may guide you through each day of your life.

- Forward Movement's website, www.forwardmovement. org, offers many resources for learning more about the Bible and engaging scripture. This includes several books in the Bible Challenge series, including each of the four gospels and *The Social Justice Bible Challenge*.

- In addition, you can find a list of resources at www. thecenterforbiblicalstudies.org. The Center for Biblical Studies also offers a Read the Bible in a Year program and reading plans for the New Testament, Psalms, and Proverbs.

- Once you've finished one complete reading of the Bible, start over and do it again. God may speak differently to you in each reading. Follow the example of U.S. President John Adams, who read through the Bible each year during his adult life. We highly advocate this practice.

We are thrilled that you are participating in The Bible Challenge. May God richly bless you as you prayerfully engage the scriptures each day.

Introduction to The Acts of the Apostles

As its preface indicates, the Book of Acts is a companion volume to the Gospel according to Luke. It recounts the growth of what it calls "the Way," the community of Jesus' disciples as they spread from Jerusalem to the far corners of the world and to the heart of the Roman Empire. The account falls into two major segments. The first, Acts 1-12, focuses on the believers in Jerusalem from the resurrection of Jesus until the death of Herod Agrippa I in 44 CE, a time frame of about fourteen years. In this segment, the figure of Saint Peter looms large. The second segment, Acts 13-28, describes the expansion of the Christian movement into Asia Minor and Greece under the leadership of Saint Paul. This segment describes Paul's missionary journeys in detail, and ends with Paul under arrest in Rome, his fate uncertain. Since Paul probably died in the persecution of Christians by the Roman emperor Nero in 65 CE, the time frame for this segment is about twenty years.

In offering its account of the first generation of the Christian movement, Acts emphasizes certain key themes. It suggests that the movement developed under the guidance of the Holy Spirit, who intervenes in a spectacular way at Pentecost (2:4) and in both dramatic and more subtle ways throughout the narrative. The Jesus Movement also progressed in a coherent and orderly way, with due regard for apostolic authority. Christians faced opposition from opponents, particularly some Jewish leaders, although others, including leading Pharisees, were more sympathetic. The movement also encountered Roman authorities, although on every occasion where some verdict is rendered, Christians are judged to be innocent of any political threat to the empire.

The Beginning of the Movement in Jerusalem: Acts 1-12

The story of the early community begins with the ascension of Jesus, now placed forty days after the resurrection. This is different from the end of the Gospel of Luke, which places the ascension immediately after Jesus' resurrection. Immediately after the ascension, the remaining eleven apostles pick a successor to Judas: Matthias, who is not heard from again. The Twelve, along with other followers of Jesus, remain silent until the advent of the Holy Spirit at Pentecost. Inspired preaching brings converts and the community develops, caring for one another in a model fashion. The apostles continue the mission of Jesus by healing a lame man, an action that antagonizes the authorities. The idealized picture of the community, sharing all their worldly goods, is repeated. Yet there are divisions, including disciples who try to deceive the apostles. They receive their due punishment. The basic pattern is repeated. The apostles continue their wondrous mission and are then arrested for it, but freed for more preaching.

A major development in the life of the church is the appointment of seven "deacons" to serve the needs of Greek-speaking believers. One of them, Stephen, is an ardent preacher whose sermon critical of the temple leads to his execution. The death of the proto-martyr, who was filled with the Holy Spirit, does not stymie the movement. Instead, one of Stephen's fellow deacons, Philip, engages in a mission to the Samaritans. This mission expands further when Philip encounters a royal official, a eunuch, from Ethiopia. Although an Ethiopian might count as a Gentile, this eunuch knows his Jewish scriptures; he is reading Isaiah as he is being transported home. Philip interprets the passage from Isaiah, and the eunuch seeks baptism. By the end of this story, two groups of people loosely associated with Jewish traditions—but people who had probably been circumcised—have joined the community of faith.

Seeds of further growth are sown in chapter 9 with the conversion of Saul, the former persecutor, but Peter's activity dominates the next chapters. He continues his miraculous ministry, healing and even raising the dead. Of equal importance is his missionary work, which brings him, guided by spirit-induced visions, to Caesarea and the home of the Roman centurion Cornelius. There, the Holy Spirit is poured out on the Gentiles. The event is so significant that it is repeated in a report by Peter to the community in Jerusalem.

The account of the early days includes a report of the church in Antioch, where believers were first called Christians. That community showed its solidarity with the church in Jerusalem by sending aid in the hands of Barnabas and Saul at a time of famine. This portion of the story ends with another look at Jerusalem, where the church suffers persecution under Herod Agrippa I, leading to the martyrdom of James, son of Zebedee, and another arrest of Peter, who is miraculously released. Herod, the persecutor, dies a horrible death, duly deserved in the view of Acts, while the gospel continues to spread.

Continuity of the Movement

The concern for the orderly development of the movement is evident from the first episodes of Acts. What is important in the story of the choice of Matthias is the integrity of the group of the Twelve, authoritative witnesses of the life, death, and resurrection of Jesus. It is on the foundation of this group that the Church rests.

Concern for the proper line of authority is also evident in the story of the selection of the first deacons. Acts reports that there were complaints from the "Hellenists," probably Greek-speaking Jewish Christians, about the ways in which their "widows" were being treated. On the recommendation of the community, the apostles appointed seven men, all with Greek names, to provide for the community's needs. The account suggests that these deacons were in a subordinate position to the apostles, whose primary responsibility was to preach, although it is clear from Stephen's story in Acts 7 that the deacons did more than serve at table. It is likely that the account tidies up what was a complex situation and emphasizes the hierarchical role of the apostolic leadership.

A similar concern surfaces in the account of the spread of the new faith beyond the boundaries of the Jewish community in Philip's mission to the Samaritans. The enthusiastic reception of his message by the Samaritans is incomplete until the Jerusalem community sends the apostles Peter and John. While the Samaritans had been baptized in the name of Jesus, they had not received the Holy Spirit, which only happened when the apostles laid hands on them. Yet the Holy Spirit can also take the initiative, as it does when Gentiles are first brought into the community.

The account of a conversion of a Roman military officer, a paradigm case of a Gentile convert, drives home the principle of apostolic authority even further. Acts 10 tells the story of Cornelius, centurion of the Italian cohort stationed in Caesarea, a devout man who readily gave alms and prayed constantly. Cornelius has an angelic vision bidding him to fetch Peter who was visiting nearby Joppa. At the same time, Peter has a vision in which he sees an invitation to a very nonkosher picnic being served by birds from heaven, which he understands to be an invitation to accept Gentiles into the community. Peter and Cornelius meet, and the centurion joins the movement. The elaborate and dramatic tale provides some indication of the importance of welcoming Gentiles into the expanding movement. The episode's significance is reinforced by Peter's retelling of his revelatory vision in Jerusalem when the "circumcision party" objects to his welcoming of non-Jews.

The mission to the Gentiles was in fact based in large part on Paul's activity. Paul understood himself to be the "apostle to the Gentiles" while Peter had been assigned to be the "apostle to the circumcised." For the author of Acts, an important point is that Peter, a leading apostle of the Jerusalem community, was the first to engage in outreach to the Gentiles, extended under the guidance of the Holy Spirit. Paul was simply following in the footsteps of the leaders of the Jerusalem church.

The Spread of the Gospel to Rome: Acts 13-28

Acts introduces Paul, still named Saul, into the narrative in Acts 7, when he assisted in the execution of the deacon Stephen. Paul went on to persecute early Christians and was sent on a mission from the high priest in Jerusalem to Jews in Damascus. On the way there, he has a dramatic encounter with the risen Jesus, who famously asks why Paul is persecuting him. Blinded by the encounter, Paul is led to Damascus where he encounters a Christian disciple, Ananias. Guided by a divine vision, Ananias instructs Paul in the faith and baptizes him. After that experience, Paul, now an apostle for the new faith, engages in missionary activity. Facing opposition from the Jews, he escapes from Damascus, lowered from the wall in a basket. Acts thus reflects the historical fact that Paul was an early advocate of missionary activity, but the main responsibility for outreach to the Gentiles rests with Peter.

In the second half of Acts, the figure of Paul looms large. Acts organizes its account of his missionary work into three missionary journeys, followed by a report of his time in Jerusalem. After his arrest there and several dramatic speeches, Paul, under arrest, sets sail on a harrowing journey. The book ends with Paul under house arrest in Rome, preaching and defending his gospel message.

In the first missionary journey, the community at Antioch sends Paul and Barnabas on the road. They travel first to the island of Cyprus, and then to the southern coast of Asia Minor, now Turkey, where they visit various cities—Perga in Pamphylia, Antioch in Pisidia, Iconium, and Lystra—before returning to their home base in Syrian Antioch.

Between the first and second missionary journeys, Acts reports an important meeting that addressed a major controversy in the early years of the Church. We know from Paul's own correspondence, particularly the epistle to the Galatians, that his relationship with other early missionaries was sometimes tense. How Gentiles were to be integrated into the new community of believers in Christ was a point of controversy. Were they required to be circumcised? Did they have to observe distinctive Jewish dietary and purity laws? Paul's own position was clear: Gentiles were to be accepted as Gentiles. It was faith in Christ and that alone that established their relationship with God. Circumcision and kashrut laws were matters of indifference.

Acts 15 reports this controversy and its resolution between the stories of Paul's first and second missionary journeys. The same kind of concern for order that characterized the early chapters of Acts is evident here as well. A controversy in Antioch about whether Gentiles should be required to accept circumcision prompts the community to send Paul and Barnabas to Jerusalem. There, in a formal assembly of the community, some members, particularly adherents of the Pharisaic tradition, argue that Gentiles should be circumcised. Peter responds with a speech citing the experience of the early Church that had welcomed Gentiles into its midst and arguing, in good Pauline fashion, that they are "saved by grace." The climax of the event is a speech in which James cites Amos 9:11-12 to support his position that "other peoples…even all the Gentiles" (Acts 15:17) may seek the Lord. The position defended by Peter and James wins the day, and the assembly issues a formal letter, with language echoing classical political decrees, that Gentiles do not have to be circumcised. According to this decree, they do, however, have to abide by some minimum regard for Jewish concerns by abstaining from "what has been sacrificed to idols and from blood and from what is strangled and from fornication" (Acts 15:29). How the details of that decree relate to the practices evidenced in Paul's letters (e.g., 1 Corinthians 8:10 on "eating food sacrificed to idols") is a long-standing issue, although it does seem that there was general agreement that Gentiles could become members of the faith community without circumcision.

In the second major journey, Paul revisits his initial mission territory in Asia Minor, now with new fellow workers. Barnabas had returned to Cyprus, and his place had been taken by Silas. In Lystra, Paul takes on another associate, a young man of a Jewish mother and a Gentile father, Timothy, who will loom large in Paul's subsequent endeavors. With his new team in place, Paul heeds a visionary summons to leave behind Asia Minor and to travel across the Bosporus. Paul and his co-workers travel to Macedonia, north of Greece. There they evangelize the cities of Philippi, Thessalonica, and Berea before heading to the heart of Greece, to Athens and Corinth. Finally, Paul returns to his home base in Syrian Antioch.

Acts says little about Paul's stay at Antioch and has him travel back immediately to the Aegean area by way of former mission territories, Pamphylia and Galatia, in the heart of Asia Minor. Thereafter Paul makes his headquarters in Ephesus, a city he visited briefly on his return from Greece. Ephesus becomes the center of the "third missionary journey" (18:24-19:41), an important period in Paul's life when he probably composed his major epistles, Galatians, 1 and 2 Corinthians, and Romans. From Ephesus he returns once more to mainland Greece before heading back to Jerusalem. On the way he stops at Miletus to address the elders of Ephesus who had come to bid him farewell. The third journey ends in Jerusalem.

After the conclusion of the three missionary journeys, with Paul finally in Jerusalem, the pace of the narrative changes. The next chapters narrate several events: a disturbance in the temple that leads to Paul's arrest, a plot to kill Paul, his removal from Jerusalem to Caesarea, his appeal to Caesar, the consultation between the Roman governor Festus and the Jewish king Agrippa, and the final disposition of his case in Caesarea. Within these brief narrative blocks come long speeches that fill most of the account. Once Paul is sent on his way to Rome, the action resumes with a vivid description of a storm at sea, which causes a shipwreck from which Paul is saved. A brief episode on the island of Malta shows Paul still in divine favor. From there, Paul is brought to Rome, where, under arrest, he meets with Jewish leaders and preaches to them, apparently unsuccessfully.

Speeches and Their Message

One striking feature of Acts for a modern reader is the large number of speeches appearing throughout the story. Acts is hardly unique in this regard, since historians from the time of Thucydides had created speeches for their leading characters to shape and interpret the narrative.

Peter's voice is heard often in the first chapters of Acts, explaining the need to replace Judas, preaching at Pentecost, preaching after healing a cripple in Solomon's Portico, defending the movement before the Sanhedrin, in dialogue with the wayward disciples Ananias and Sapphira, and again defending his faith before the Sanhedrin. Among all of these, the impressive speech at Pentecost conveys a particularly strong theological message. It argues that Jesus, made Lord and Christ by his resurrection from the dead, has fulfilled prophecy, and the speech summons hearers to repent and be baptized. Another set of striking Christological affirmations appears in Peter's third speech in Solomon's Portico, where he describes Jesus as the servant of God, echoing Isaiah 52:13, and labels him the "author of life," foreseen Messiah, and, echoing Deuteronomy 18:15-19, a prophet like Moses.

The longest speech in Acts, found in chapter 7, belongs to Stephen. Sounding like a prophet of old, he offers a comprehensive account of salvation history, tracing God's interaction with Abraham, Joseph, and Moses. Following the lead of the biblical historians, he recounts stories of Israel's idolatry, both during the Exodus and beyond. He has particularly harsh words for the temple, whose construction he argues was contrary to the will of the God for whom "heaven is my throne" (Isaiah 66:1-2). He agrees that the Law was delivered by angels but is not obeyed by his audience, an accusation that does not win him friends.

In the second half of Acts, some of the other apostles make cameo appearances. Thus the pivotal Apostolic Council features two rather brief speeches by Peter (Acts 15:7-11) and James (15:13-21). Yet overall, this portion of Acts resounds with Paul's voice, first preaching to Gentiles in Pisidian Antioch, then, in a much more sophisticated fashion, to Athenians on the historic Areopagus, or Mars' Hill. In each of these speeches, Paul, like well-trained ancient orators, adapts to his audience to make his case. In the Areopagus speech, he interprets a dedicatory inscription and cites the well-known Hellenistic poet

Aratus to win over the educated crowd, though with only limited success.

Paul's next speech, to the elders of Ephesus at Miletus, delivered on his way to Jerusalem, has a different tone, offering consolation while warning of dangers to come. His final speeches (before the Sanhedrin; before Felix, the Roman governor of Judaea; and before Herod Agrippa II, the Jewish monarch who did not control Judaea but had authority over the temple) echo the kinds of rhetoric at home in forensic or legal settings. One interesting move that Paul makes in two of these speeches is to cite his own experience of encounter with the resurrected Christ on the road to Damascus. Each report has slight variations, as one might expect in oral delivery. Again, acting like a good rhetorician, Paul even alludes to a famous line from a play of Euripides, now set on the lips of the resurrected Jesus. Paul's speeches defend the gospel outlined in Peter's early speeches, but they also show Paul to be a faithful apostle, and not a political revolutionary.

Engaging Stories

Acts is an account that is meant to instruct its Christian audience, to reinforce certain fundamental claims about who Christ is, how the community of disciples functions under the guidance of the Holy Spirit, and how this community does not pose a political threat to the Roman order. At the same time, Acts is a story that engages and entertains its readers. Sometimes it does so with apparent literary sophistication, as in the portrait of Paul as an orator, in the allusions to Aratus and Euripides. Sometimes its moves are subtler and more humorous. The story of Peter, miraculously delivered from prison and knocking at the door of the house of Mary of Jerusalem while the maid Rhoda in her amazement fails to respond, resembles the kind of scene one might encounter in comic drama. Another story recounts

Paul's resurrection of Eutychus ("Lucky"), a young man who dozed off while Paul was preaching in Troas, fell from a third-story window, and died. The story would no doubt recall for ancient readers a similar tale from Homer's *Odyssey*, when Odysseus in Hades meets one of his crew, Elpenor, who had fallen from a ladder after a night of drinking.

The variety of scenes depicted in Acts also affirms its literary artistry. These include fiery tongues of fire descending on frightened apostles; prison breaks; grisly deaths, both good and bad; resurrections from the dead; contests with magicians and exorcists; a public assembly in tumult; a fierce storm at sea; and numerous "courtroom" scenes where Peter and Paul defend themselves and their community with well-formed orations. With the literary echoes that some of these scenes display, the whole lot presents a tapestry of engaging narrative. As noted scholar Richard Pervo puts it, Acts is a work that provides "profit with delight."

Story, History, and Faith

While Acts displays many techniques and motifs of popular narrative, the book also is telling an important historical story. The followers of a man executed as a political criminal did not fade into historical obscurity. They maintained their fellowship, came to understand the death and renewed life of their master Jesus through the aid of Israel's scriptures, and engaged in an effort to convince one and all, Jew and Gentile alike, that through their master the God of Israel was doing something new for all humankind. The mission involved conflict, internal and external, both of which Acts reports but minimizes. The mission progressed in the hands of leaders whose insight and tenacity helped the community to hold together and grow. Acts captures some of their struggle, while it paints an idealized portrait of their leadership and their relations.

The author of Acts has sources. These include the oral tradition of people who lived through the thirty-five-year period that it relates. The author may also know the letters of Paul, although it does not say anything about them or about Paul as a writer. The author may have a travel record from a companion of Paul, which may lie behind the "we" passages that appear in connection with the third missionary journey. But Acts is not the work of a modern critical historian. It is, like so much of the account of the past in scripture, an appeal to faith, a summons to see in the drama of history the hand of God mysteriously but resolutely at work.

Professor Harry Attridge
Sterling Professor of Divinity
Yale Divinity School
New Haven, Connecticut

A Journey Through Acts

The 50 Day Bible Challenge

Acts 1:1-11

1 In the first book, Theophilus, I wrote about all that Jesus did and taught from the beginning ²until the day when he was taken up to heaven, after giving instructions through the Holy Spirit to the apostles whom he had chosen. ³After his suffering he presented himself alive to them by many convincing proofs, appearing to them during forty days and speaking about the kingdom of God. ⁴While staying with them, he ordered them not to leave Jerusalem, but to wait there for the promise of the Father. "This," he said, "is what you have heard from me; ⁵for John baptized with water, but you will be baptized with the Holy Spirit not many days from now."

⁶So when they had come together, they asked him, "Lord, is this the time when you will restore the kingdom to Israel?" ⁷He replied, "It is not for you to know the times or periods that the Father has set by his own authority. ⁸But you will receive power when the Holy Spirit has come upon you; and you will be my witnesses in Jerusalem, in all Judea and Samaria, and to the ends of the earth." ⁹When he had said this, as they were watching, he was lifted up, and a cloud took him out of their sight. ¹⁰While he was going and they were gazing up toward heaven, suddenly two men in white robes stood by them. ¹¹They said, "Men of Galilee, why do you stand looking up toward heaven? This Jesus, who has been taken up from you into heaven, will come in the same way as you saw him go into heaven."

Reflection

This passage is read on the feast of the Ascension and occasionally on Easter. As the prologue to the book of Acts, Luke writes to Theophilus tying together "all that Jesus did" with all that God through the Holy Spirit is about to do. The Book of Acts is about the power of the Holy Spirit sending out the apostles to undertake God's mission.

Luke roots the story of Christianity in the Abrahamic tradition. He understands that those who first preached the gospel in Jesus' name were part of a great narrative arc that began with the creation story. Through the ministry of the apostles, God wishes to be reconciled to the world and partners with humanity to bring peace to all.

Luke also understands this mission as the great and surprising restoration of the kingdom of Israel. Jesus taught us that this was not a political kingdom that would mimic the reigning powers of violence. Instead, Luke grasps that the kingdom of God has expanded in and through Jesus Christ to include all people. In Christ, all people are on a mission, just as Abraham and Sarah were on a mission. We are to be a blessing to the world. We are to create communities of peace that reflect God's shalom. God has a vision that the reign of peace be given to all people in every land and that Jesus' apostles be sent to proclaim this good news.

The Rt. Rev. C. Andrew Doyle
IX Bishop of the Diocese of Texas
Houston, Texas

Questions

When do you experience the presence of the Holy Spirit? Does the experience leave you feeling more comforted or challenged?

Filled with the Holy Spirit, the apostles responded to God's mission by creating communities of peace. How do you feel called to create communities of peace in your own life?

Prayer

Lord Jesus Christ, you called your first apostles to undertake God's mission and to bring peace to all. Fill us with the gift of the Holy Spirit, giving us both wisdom to hear your voice and courage to heed the call. *Amen.*

Acts 1:12-26

¹²Then they returned to Jerusalem from the mount called Olivet, which is near Jerusalem, a sabbath day's journey away. ¹³When they had entered the city, they went to the room upstairs where they were staying, Peter, and John, and James, and Andrew, Philip and Thomas, Bartholomew and Matthew, James son of Alphaeus, and Simon the Zealot, and Judas son of James. ¹⁴All these were constantly devoting themselves to prayer, together with certain women, including Mary the mother of Jesus, as well as his brothers.

¹⁵In those days Peter stood up among the believers (together the crowd numbered about one hundred twenty persons) and said, ¹⁶"Friends, the scripture had to be fulfilled, which the Holy Spirit through David foretold concerning Judas, who became a guide for those who arrested Jesus—¹⁷for he was numbered among us and was allotted his share in this ministry." ¹⁸(Now this man acquired a field with the reward of his wickedness; and falling headlong, he burst open in the middle and all his bowels gushed out. ¹⁹This became known to all the residents of Jerusalem, so that the field was called in their language Hakeldama, that is, Field of Blood.) ²⁰"For it is written in the book of Psalms,

'Let his homestead become desolate,
    and let there be no one to live in it';

and

'Let another take his position of overseer.'

²¹So one of the men who have accompanied us during all the time that the Lord Jesus went in and out among us, ²²beginning from the baptism of John until

the day when he was taken up from us—one of these must become a witness with us to his resurrection." [23]So they proposed two, Joseph called Barsabbas, who was also known as Justus, and Matthias. [24]Then they prayed and said, "Lord, you know everyone's heart. Show us which one of these two you have chosen [25]to take the place in this ministry and apostleship from which Judas turned aside to go to his own place." [26]And they cast lots for them, and the lot fell on Matthias; and he was added to the eleven apostles.

Reflection

The story of humanity has been plagued by systems of violence since the very beginning. The mimetic and repetitive violence between siblings is a recurring motif in scripture, bringing about the destruction of families, friendships, and even whole societies. We even find arguing brothers among Jesus' own disciples as they violently compete to be considered the greatest in God's kingdom (see Luke 22:24; Mark 9:33-37).

Perhaps the most obvious biblical example of one man's violent destruction is seen in Judas Iscariot. Judas was a close friend of Jesus. They sat next to one another at the Last Supper, sharing a cup, bread, and dipping oils. Judas also had the most trusted position in the group as the keeper of the common purse. In the end, Judas was dissatisfied with the direction the Jesus movement was taking. Peace over violent revolution, love over social reform, and weakness overcoming power were not theologies that made sense to Judas. As a result, Judas betrayed his brother, bringing about the Messiah's death.

The good news of the gospel is that the Messiah's death is precisely where violence is overthrown by peace, love, and sacrifice. The victory and sting of mimetic violence is over because of Jesus' complete pacification of it.

In the wake of the resurrection, Judas is replaced. The Jerusalem church saw the continuation of the Twelve as essential. All hands were needed. They believed that they and their community had been chosen for God's mission to build new communities of peace. They were participants in the great prophetic realization of a reign of shalom prophesied by Isaiah. Jesus' death and resurrection brought about a kingdom where the lion and the lamb lie down together. God's unconditional pronouncement of peace was universal. It was meant for all people. All hands are needed for God to write a new story and undo a rivalry that has plagued humanity from the beginning of time.

The Rt. Rev. C. Andrew Doyle
IX Bishop of the Diocese of Texas
Houston, Texas

Questions

What recurring violence do you experience in life? How does it distract you from understanding and fulfilling the work of God?

Verse 14 tells us that the community, including certain women, were constantly in prayer. What role does prayer have in putting an end to violence? Why do you think Luke explicitly mentions the presence of the women?

Prayer

Loving God, you know all too well our tendency to succumb to competition, violence, and war. Overthrow our destructive ways by infusing us with that same spirit of peace, love, and sacrifice that we see in Jesus' cross, and use our hands to write a new story of shalom on this earth. In Jesus' name, *Amen.*

Acts 2:1-13

2 When the day of Pentecost had come, they were all together in one place. ²And suddenly from heaven there came a sound like the rush of a violent wind, and it filled the entire house where they were sitting. ³Divided tongues, as of fire, appeared among them, and a tongue rested on each of them. ⁴All of them were filled with the Holy Spirit and began to speak in other languages, as the Spirit gave them ability.

⁵Now there were devout Jews from every nation under heaven living in Jerusalem. ⁶And at this sound the crowd gathered and was bewildered, because each one heard them speaking in the native language of each.

⁷Amazed and astonished, they asked, "Are not all these who are speaking Galileans? ⁸And how is it that we hear, each of us, in our own native language? ⁹Parthians, Medes, Elamites, and residents of Mesopotamia, Judea and Cappadocia, Pontus and Asia, ¹⁰Phrygia and Pamphylia, Egypt and the parts of Libya belonging to Cyrene, and visitors from Rome, both Jews and proselytes, ¹¹Cretans and Arabs—in our own languages we hear them speaking about God's deeds of power." ¹²All were amazed and perplexed, saying to one another, "What does this mean?" ¹³But others sneered and said, "They are filled with new wine."

Reflection

Jesus told the disciples to stay in Jerusalem and wait for the Holy Spirit. When the Holy Spirit arrived on the day of Pentecost, the Spirit showed up with the special effects of a blockbuster film. The Spirit's entrance was rowdy, loud, and unpredictable. Like a violent wind or fire, the Spirit came with divided tongues. The Spirit's outpouring on the community produced a cacophony of languages filled with the saltiest regional dialects and idioms.

And while on the surface of things the Spirit's outpouring divided the community, on a deeper level the Spirit united them. For perhaps the first time, the community heard the message of salvation at the same time *together*. The Holy Spirit empowered the disciples to make the gospel intelligible to all people, through all languages. Whatever barrier prevented a person from communicating or hearing the gospel was dissolved by the gift of tongues. And that was the point: to empower the disciples to communicate God's love to all people.

In baptism, we are sealed by the Holy Spirit and marked as Christ's own forever. Yet, many of us struggle with our relationship to the Holy Spirit—a spontaneous-raucous person of the Trinity who is hard to pin down (quite literally!) or relate to. Yet the Spirit is the one who brings order out of chaos. The Spirit hovered over the formless earth and loved it into ordered creation. And this is precisely what the Spirit did on the day of Pentecost: loved a ragtag group of disciples into becoming the first church. How might the Spirit love us, in today's chaos, into something new?

The Rev. Elizabeth R. Costello
Associate Rector St. Thomas' Episcopal Church, Whitemarsh
Chaplain to the St. Thomas' Nursery School
Fort Washington, Pennsylvania

Questions _____

What is your relationship to the Holy Spirit? How can we invite the Spirit to make a home in our lives?

What barriers impede our ability to communicate the gospel? What new language do we need the Holy Spirit to give us in order to share God's love today?

Prayer _____

Holy Spirit, who loves us into being, who empowers us to speak with tongues of fire, and who, when we are in trouble, intercedes for us with sighs too deep for words, inflame our hearts with your love so we might burn brightly anew. In the name of the Triune God: Father, Son, and Holy Spirit. *Amen.*

Acts 2:14-36

¹⁴But Peter, standing with the eleven, raised his voice and addressed them, "Men of Judea and all who live in Jerusalem, let this be known to you, and listen to what I say. ¹⁵Indeed, these are not drunk, as you suppose, for it is only nine o'clock in the morning. ¹⁶No, this is what was spoken through the prophet Joel:

¹⁷'In the last days it will be,
        God declares,
    that I will pour out my
            Spirit upon all flesh,
        and your sons and your
            daughters shall
            prophesy,
    and your young men shall
            see visions,
        and your old men shall
            dream dreams.
¹⁸Even upon my slaves,
        both men and
        women,
    in those days I will pour
        out my Spirit;
    and they shall prophesy.

¹⁹And I will show portents
        in the heaven above
    and signs on the earth
        below,
        blood, and fire, and
            smoky mist.
²⁰The sun shall be turned
        to darkness
    and the moon to blood,
    before the coming of
        the Lord's great and
        glorious day.
²¹Then everyone who calls
        on the name of the
        Lord shall be saved.'

²²"You that are Israelites, listen to what I have to say: Jesus of Nazareth, a man attested to you by God with deeds of power, wonders, and signs that God did through him among you, as you yourselves know— ²³this man, handed over to you according to the definite plan and foreknowledge of God, you crucified and killed by the hands

of those outside the law. ²⁴But God raised him up, having freed him from death, because it was impossible for him to be held in its power. ²⁵For David says concerning him,

'I saw the Lord always
before me,
for he is at my right hand
so that I will not be
shaken;
²⁶therefore my heart was
glad, and my tongue
rejoiced;
moreover my flesh will
live in hope.
²⁷For you will not abandon
my soul to Hades,
or let your Holy One
experience
corruption.
²⁸You have made known to
me the ways of life;
you will make me full of
gladness with your
presence.'

²⁹"Fellow Israelites, I may say to you confidently of our ancestor David that he both died and was buried, and his tomb is with us to this day. ³⁰Since he was a prophet, he knew that God had sworn with an oath to him that he would put one of his descendants on his throne. ³¹Foreseeing this, David spoke of the resurrection of the Messiah, saying,

'He was not abandoned to
Hades,
nor did his flesh experience
corruption.'

³²This Jesus God raised up, and of that all of us are witnesses. ³³Being therefore exalted at the right hand of God, and having received from the Father the promise of the Holy Spirit, he has poured out this that you both see and hear. ³⁴For David did not ascend into the heavens, but he himself says,

'The Lord said to my Lord,
"Sit at my right hand,
³⁵until I make your
enemies your
footstool." '

³⁶Therefore let the entire house of Israel know with certainty that God has made him both Lord and Messiah, this Jesus whom you crucified."

Reflection

Standing with the rest of the disciples, Peter preaches his heart out to the crowd. He tells the story of Jesus: the long awaited Messiah, the fulfillment of prophetic promise, the very presence of God on earth confirmed and continued by the Holy Spirit's outpouring.

Peter tells the story that changed his life. The story that made him drop his net at Bethsaida, the story that gave him a new name, the story that he simply could not shake even on his most doubt-filled days. Peter tells the story knowing that he is part of the story. He realizes that he is not just an observer and narrator but an actor in the unfolding drama of God's salvation. Spirit-filled on the best of days to proclaim Jesus as the Messiah, human enough on the worst of days to deny knowing Jesus, and loved enough to be named the rock of the church: Peter cannot stop telling the story.

In baptism, we are initiated into God's story. Each day we wake up and find ourselves part of God's still-unfolding redemptive plan. Pentecost reminds us that God's story does not stop with Jesus' crucifixion and resurrection but continues through God's mission embodied by the church. As our church continues to live out the story, we cannot help but follow in Peter's footsteps. This story continues to call us to drop our nets of privilege, fear, guilt, or whatever prevents us from following Jesus. As we drop our nets to follow Jesus, as we continue to be transformed in that very process, we cannot help but be like Peter, sharing the story that continues to save.

The Rev. Elizabeth R. Costello
Associate Rector St. Thomas' Episcopal Church, Whitemarsh
Chaplain to the St. Thomas' Nursery School
Fort Washington, Pennsylvania

Questions _____

Who first shared God's story with you? How did it go? If you were to share God's story with a neighbor, what would your angle be?

How does the church proclaim God's story through action in the liturgy and public witness?

Prayer _____

Heavenly Father, we thank you for loving us into existence and for redeeming us through your Son Jesus Christ. Empower us with your life-giving Spirit to share your love story for all of creation through the gifts that you have given us and through the way we live our lives. *Amen.*

Acts 2:37-47

37Now when they heard this, they were cut to the heart and said to Peter and to the other apostles, "Brothers, what should we do?" 38Peter said to them, "Repent, and be baptized every one of you in the name of Jesus Christ so that your sins may be forgiven; and you will receive the gift of the Holy Spirit. 39For the promise is for you, for your children, and for all who are far away, everyone whom the Lord our God calls to him." 40And he testified with many other arguments and exhorted them, saying, "Save yourselves from this corrupt generation." 41So those who welcomed his message were baptized, and that day about three thousand persons were added.

42They devoted themselves to the apostles' teaching and fellowship, to the breaking of bread and the prayers.

43Awe came upon everyone, because many wonders and signs were being done by the apostles. 44All who believed were together and had all things in common; 45they would sell their possessions and goods and distribute the proceeds to all, as any had need. 46Day by day, as they spent much time together in the temple, they broke bread at home and ate their food with glad and generous hearts, 47praising God and having the goodwill of all the people. And day by day the Lord added to their number those who were being saved.

Reflection

In this passage, we see some of the first converts to Christianity. These new followers asked, "What must we do?" Peter's answer: "Repent, and be baptized." The outcome from following these two commandments was salvation. However, once people were saved, an ongoing commitment to Christ's teachings was vital. They needed to study the scriptures, be in fellowship with one another, and be devoted to worship, where they broke bread with one another and offered prayers praising God.

Two thousand years later, it is the same formula. We are saved by our baptisms. And yet to enjoy the full gift of salvation, we need to live in community with one another, we need to study the Word of God, we need to break bread with one another and pray for one another. Repenting and being baptized are the easiest parts of the equation. Obedience and commitment are much harder. We get distracted. Maybe work dominates our lives. Perhaps the church we joined disappoints us. And then, we fall away, missing out on the joy our Lord intends for us, the joy that comes from fellowship with other Christians struggling along the same path. Christ intends for us to be in community with one another where we share one another's lives and problems, joys and fears. Church is the community where we can bear one another's burdens and grow into the full stature of Christ. Recommit yourself today to the formula that has worked for thousands of years.

The Rev. Melissa Hollerith
Former Chaplain, St. Christopher's School
Richmond, Virginia

The Very Rev. Randolph Marshall Hollerith
Dean, Washington National Cathedral
Washington, D.C.

Questions _____

What obstacles in your life prevent you from being obedient in the study of the scriptures?

What obstacles prevent you from being committed to a worship life in the church?

Ask someone to pray for you as you recommit your life to being obedient and devoted to the teachings of Christ.

Prayer _____

Heavenly Father, give us the gift of an obedient heart. We know the joy that awaits us each day from walking closer with you in the scriptures and in church. Draw near and remind us of this wonderful gift and give us the strength to recommit our lives to you. *Amen.*

Acts 3:1-26

3 One day Peter and John were going up to the temple at the hour of prayer, at three o'clock in the afternoon. ²And a man lame from birth was being carried in. People would lay him daily at the gate of the temple called the Beautiful Gate so that he could ask for alms from those entering the temple. ³When he saw Peter and John about to go into the temple, he asked them for alms. ⁴Peter looked intently at him, as did John, and said, "Look at us." ⁵And he fixed his attention on them, expecting to receive something from them. ⁶But Peter said, "I have no silver or gold, but what I have I give you; in the name of Jesus Christ of Nazareth, stand up and walk." ⁷And he took him by the right hand and raised him up; and immediately his feet and ankles were made strong. ⁸Jumping up, he stood and began to walk, and he entered the temple with them,

walking and leaping and praising God. ⁹All the people saw him walking and praising God, ¹⁰and they recognized him as the one who used to sit and ask for alms at the Beautiful Gate of the temple; and they were filled with wonder and amazement at what had happened to him. ¹¹While he clung to Peter and John, all the people ran together to them in the portico called Solomon's Portico, utterly astonished. ¹²When Peter saw it, he addressed the people, "You Israelites, why do you wonder at this, or why do you stare at us, as though by our own power or piety we had made him walk? ¹³The God of Abraham, the God of Isaac, and the God of Jacob, the God of our ancestors has glorified his servant Jesus, whom you handed over and rejected in the presence of Pilate, though he had decided to release him. ¹⁴But you rejected the Holy and Righteous One and asked to have a murderer given to you, [15]and you killed the Author of life, whom God raised from the dead. To this we are witnesses. [16]And by faith in his name, his name itself has made this man strong, whom you see and know; and the faith that is through Jesus has given him this perfect health in the presence of all of you.

[17]"And now, friends, I know that you acted in ignorance, as did also your rulers. [18]In this way God fulfilled what he had foretold through all the prophets, that his Messiah would suffer. [19]Repent therefore, and turn to God so that your sins may be wiped out, [20]so that times of refreshing may come from the presence of the Lord, and that he may send the Messiah appointed for you, that is, Jesus, [21]who must remain in heaven until the time of universal restoration that God announced long ago through his holy prophets. [22]Moses said, 'The Lord your God will raise up for you from your own people a prophet like me. You must listen to whatever he tells you. [23]And it will be that everyone who does not listen to that prophet will be utterly rooted out of the people.' [24]And all the prophets, as many as have spoken, from Samuel and those after him, also predicted these days. [25]You are the descendants of the prophets and of the covenant that God gave to your ancestors, saying to Abraham, 'And in your descendants all the families of the earth shall be blessed.' [26]When God raised up his servant, he sent him first to you, to bless you by turning each of you from your wicked ways."

Reflection

In this passage, we have a miraculous healing by the disciples Peter and John. The lame man in front of the temple gate begs for alms each day. When Peter and John approach the temple gate, the lame man hopes to receive alms from them, but instead he receives what they have been commissioned to share—God's healing power. And behold, the lame man is able to stand, his feet and legs suddenly function; he can walk and leap. All who witness this miracle are astounded. And Peter takes this moment to tell them they should not be surprised. Peter reminds them that the God of Abraham, Isaac, and Jacob sent his son Jesus, and they rejected him and had him killed. But it is Jesus who heals. And because of this lame man's faith in Jesus, he has been made strong and well.

In his exhortation, Peter is hopeful that those at the temple will awaken to the knowledge that Jesus heals, that Jesus is the Messiah they hoped for but rejected. Peter as a faithful disciple hopes to turn their hearts to the One in whose name they heal others. Isn't it always that way? When we need to convince folks about something, we need to produce data, facts, evidence, and proof. I wonder how many who saw the lame man healed became believers that day?

There is a reason that Jesus says, "Blessed are those who have not seen and yet have believed" (John 20:29). May we never lose faith in the healing power of Jesus simply because we have not seen a healing.

The Rev. Melissa Hollerith
Former Chaplain, St. Christopher's School
Richmond, Virginia

The Very Rev. Randolph Marshall Hollerith
Dean, Washington National Cathedral
Washington, D.C.

Questions

What would make it easier for you to have faith in Jesus' healing power? Why?

Do you think if you had been present at the temple and witnessed the lame man's healing that you would have become a follower? Why or why not?

Prayer

Heavenly Father, the man who brought his son for healing asked Jesus to help his unbelief. We all have moments of doubt. Help us to realize, as Jesus promised, that everything is possible for those who have faith. In your Holy Name we pray. *Amen.*

Acts 4:1-22

4 While Peter and John were speaking to the people, the priests, the captain of the temple, and the Sadducees came to them, ²much annoyed because they were teaching the people and proclaiming that in Jesus there is the resurrection of the dead. ³So they arrested them and put them in custody until the next day, for it was already evening. ⁴But many of those who heard the word believed; and ⸀ they numbered about five thousand.

⁵The next day their rulers, elders, and scribes assembled in Jerusalem, ⁶with Annas the high priest, Caiaphas, John, and Alexander, and all who were of the high-priestly family. ⁷When they had made the prisoners stand in their midst, they inquired, "By what power or by what name did you do this?" ⁸Then Peter, filled with the Holy Spirit, said to them, "Rulers of the people and elders, ⁹if we are questioned today because of a good deed done to someone who was sick and are asked how this man has been healed, ¹⁰let it be known to all of you, and to all the people of Israel, that this man is standing before you in good health by the name of Jesus Christ of Nazareth, whom you crucified, whom God raised from the dead. ¹¹This Jesus is

'the stone that was rejected
by you, the
builders;
it has become the
cornerstone.'

¹²There is salvation in no one else, for there is no other name under heaven given among mortals by which we must be saved."

¹³Now when they saw the boldness of Peter and John and realized that they were uneducated and ordinary men, they were amazed and recognized

them as companions of Jesus. [14]When they saw the man who had been cured standing beside them, they had nothing to say in opposition.

[15]So they ordered them to leave the council while they discussed the matter with one another. [16]They said, "What will we do with them? For it is obvious to all who live in Jerusalem that a notable sign has been done through them; we cannot deny it. [17]But to keep it from spreading further among the people, let us warn them to speak no more to anyone in this name." [18]So they called them and ordered them not to speak or teach at all in the name of Jesus. [19]But Peter and John answered them, "Whether it is right in God's sight to listen to you rather than to God, you must judge; [20]for we cannot keep from speaking about what we have seen and heard." [21]After threatening them again, they let them go, finding no way to punish them because of the people, for all of them praised God for what had happened. [22]For the man on whom this sign of healing had been performed was more than forty years old.

Reflection

Good trouble. Christians have a long and venerable tradition of resisting tyranny. (We also have a history of supporting tyrants, but that is another story for another day.) For today's reading, it is noteworthy that Peter and John have been dragged before the authorities simply for healing a man crippled from birth—all in the name of Jesus.

Of course, it was not only the healing that got them in trouble. Peter and John had also used the miracle to speak truth to power. They proclaimed Jesus the Messiah—the same Jesus who had resisted and consequently been crushed by Rome. God raised him from the dead and in so doing put a stamp of approval on his faithful witness. Having seen all this firsthand, how could Peter and John possibly be silent?

Peter and John were not special in any way. They were faithful to God, and they faithfully acted and spoke with the confidence that was given to them. Wherever we may find ourselves, God is calling us to follow their example.

The challenge, of course, is to know what is good trouble and what is just plain old trouble. May we have both the wisdom to discern and the courage to act.

Dr. David Creech
Assistant Professor of Religion, Concordia College
Moorhead, Minnesota

Questions

When was a time that you got in trouble for doing good? How did you know it was the right thing to do? How did it work itself out?

How might God be calling you to get into good trouble this week?

Prayer

God who calls us to do what is just and right, give us wisdom and courage to follow the example of Peter and John. Help us discern where you might be calling us to faithful resistance and good trouble. In Jesus' name, *Amen*.

Acts 4:23-31

²³After they were released, they went to their friends and reported what the chief priests and the elders had said to them. ²⁴When they heard it, they raised their voices together to God and said, "Sovereign Lord, who made the heaven and the earth, the sea, and everything in them, ²⁵it is you who said by the Holy Spirit through our ancestor David, your servant:

'Why did the Gentiles rage,
and the peoples imagine
vain things?
²⁶The kings of the earth
took their stand,
and the rulers have
gathered together
against the Lord and
against his Messiah.'

²⁷For in this city, in fact, both Herod and Pontius Pilate, with the Gentiles and the peoples of Israel, gathered together against your holy servant Jesus, whom you anointed, ²⁸to do whatever your hand and your plan had predestined to take place. ²⁹And now, Lord, look at their threats, and grant to your servants to speak your word with all boldness, ³⁰while you stretch out your hand to heal, and signs and wonders are performed through the name of your holy servant Jesus." ³¹When they had prayed, the place in which they were gathered together was shaken; and they were all filled with the Holy Spirit and spoke the word of God with boldness.

Reflection

The Evangelical Lutheran Church in America has a catchy little slogan: "God's work. Our hands." It is a quick reminder of how God acts in the world—our faithful response to God's calling is essential, but it is still God's work. Faithful witness to the world will always be empowered by the Holy Spirit.

Yesterday, we saw how Peter and John got into good trouble for healing a man and speaking truth to power. In today's reading, we are reminded that the good work we do is not our own. Peter and John are released with a stern warning and return to the community of believers. Confident that God had called them to the task of proclaiming Jesus but fearful from the threats of those in power, they turn to God and ask for courage to live faithfully into that call.

Their petition does not go unanswered. God moves: They are filled with the Holy Spirit and go forth to proclaim with boldness.

As we go forward in Acts, we will see that being empowered by God's Spirit does not mean that all obstacles are removed or that the task gets any easier. God's work is a high calling and often upsets accepted norms and values. Empowered by the Holy Spirit, may we use our hands to do God's work.

Dr. David Creech
Assistant Professor of Religion, Concordia College
Moorhead, Minnesota

Questions

Buildings shaken as evidence of the presence of the Holy Spirit are not common today. What might empowerment by the Holy Spirit look like today?

How do you know when it is God doing God's work with your hands?

Prayer

Empowering God, fill us with your Spirit to live out your calling in our lives faithfully. May we do your work with our hands. In Jesus' name, *Amen.*

Acts 4:32-37

³²Now the whole group of those who believed were of one heart and soul, and no one claimed private ownership of any possessions, but everything they owned was held in common. ³³With great power the apostles gave their testimony to the resurrection of the Lord Jesus, and great grace was upon them all. ³⁴There was not a needy person among them, for as many as owned lands or houses sold them and brought the proceeds of what was sold. ³⁵They laid it at the apostles' feet, and it was distributed to each as any had need. ³⁶There was a Levite, a native of Cyprus, Joseph, to whom the apostles gave the name Barnabas (which means "son of encouragement"). ³⁷He sold a field that belonged to him, then brought the money, and laid it at the apostles' feet.

Reflection

It has been expressed on more than one occasion the desire for the modern church to be more like the church in the Book of Acts. I have often wondered what exactly people mean by this desire. The early church was filled with excitement, fear, wonder, hope, and a certain sense of urgency that we may perhaps not possess in the same way. Why not? Many of us hold and know the sacred stories that have been passed down to us as precious gifts, yet far too many of us have not taken them into our hearts in a way that spurs us toward meaningful action and ongoing discipleship.

The fourth chapter of Acts is a model and an invitation to lay all that we have and all that we are at the feet of God so that our talents, passions, actions, words, and lives can be used as currency of love and purpose. It is also a reminder that goodness comes when we find a way to use what we have for more than our own prosperity. Seeking a communal sense of purpose and working toward a higher call is the heart of who we are as Christians. It is the beautiful response to Jesus' life and witness. The challenge for us is to remain open, awake, and ready to follow this call. Yet again, we live in a time of urgency. Let the example of the early church guide us in the ways we might build up the kingdom of God in our own time.

Emily Slichter-Given
Director of Parish Participation, St. Thomas' Episcopal Church, Whitemarsh Fort Washington, Pennsylvania

Questions

What would it be like to truly see our possessions and resources as gifts given for the common good of our community?

What transformational power could we bring to a broken and searching world if we simply gave of ourselves without keeping a tally sheet or expecting others to do it in our place?

How might we and those around us seek to be of one heart and soul so that together we could be the face of grace, the voice of justice, and the hands of service?

Prayer

Christ Jesus, you came among us as one who gave, loved, and served. Help us to keep our hearts and minds focused on your example so that we may do the same. Give us courage and wisdom to follow in the path of our brothers and sisters from the Book of Acts. Remind us when we forget. Show us mercy when we fall short. Give us companionship on the way and lead us in your truth, today and forevermore. *Amen.*

Acts 5:1-11

5 But a man named Ananias, with the consent of his wife Sapphira, sold a piece of property; ²with his wife's knowledge, he kept back some of the proceeds, and brought only a part and laid it at the apostles' feet. ³"Ananias," Peter asked, "why has Satan filled your heart to lie to the Holy Spirit and to keep back part of the proceeds of the land? ⁴While it remained unsold, did it not remain your own? And after it was sold, were not the proceeds at your disposal? How is it that you have contrived this deed in your heart? You did not lie to us but to God!" ⁵Now when Ananias heard these words, he fell down and died. And great fear seized all who heard of it. ⁶The young men came and wrapped up his body, then carried him out and buried him.

⁷After an interval of about three hours his wife came in, not knowing what had happened. ⁸Peter said to her, "Tell me whether you and your husband sold the land for such and such a price." And she said, "Yes, that was the price." ⁹Then Peter said to her, "How is it that you have agreed together to put the Spirit of the Lord to the test? Look, the feet of those who have buried your husband are at the door, and they will carry you out." ¹⁰Immediately she fell down at his feet and died. When the young men came in they found her dead, so they carried her out and buried her beside her husband. ¹¹And great fear seized the whole church and all who heard of these things.

Reflection

Some portions of scripture leave us with more questions than answers. What is the story of Ananias and Sapphira meant to communicate to us? It is easy to jump to the terrifying portion of the text. Will we really be struck dead if we hold back money from God? Will our lives be used as an example of how not to live? One way to approach this story is to consider how holding back from God and others might be a death of a different kind. What dies within us when we do not share our lives and our resources with God, to be used to God's glory in the world?

Finding community can be a challenge in modern times. Our busyness and emphasis on self-accomplishment are often diametrically opposed to the loving relationships and selflessness called for in the Book of Acts. The story of Ananias and Sapphira reminds us that it is difficult to commit ourselves totally to others without reservation. It can also be hard to resist the tendency to depend on ourselves instead of relying on the grace and care of God. This is often especially the case when Christians consider how generous to be with their finances. Our fear and need for self-made security can keep us from offering our resources in impactful and radical ways. The call for us is to rest in the providence and care of God as shown to us in scripture and in all the beautiful places of our lives. This clear message calls for us to give to God first—and without fear.

Emily Slichter-Given
Director of Parish Participation, St. Thomas' Episcopal Church, Whitemarsh Fort Washington, Pennsylvania

Questions _____

Do you know someone who is a model of generosity? How might you share what you have in similar ways?

What do you possess that the world dearly needs? What might you be keeping from God and others that is causing a type of death in your life?

How can you free yourself from the fear of not having enough?

Prayer _____

God of all goodness, you have given us all that we need. Help us to know this in our daily lives and to reciprocate with the same generosity. In a world of want, make us ready to respond to your people in need. Inspire us to be quick to love and willing to serve. Encourage us to be bold in our giving, open in our learning, and constant in our commitment to grow in you. *Amen.*

Acts 5:12-26

¹²Now many signs and wonders were done among the people through the apostles. And they were all together in Solomon's Portico. ¹³None of the rest dared to join them, but the people held them in high esteem. ¹⁴Yet more than ever believers were added to the Lord, great numbers of both men and women, ¹⁵so that they even carried out the sick into the streets, and laid them on cots and mats, in order that Peter's shadow might fall on some of them as he came by. ¹⁶A great number of people would also gather from the towns around Jerusalem, bringing the sick and those tormented by unclean spirits, and they were all cured.

¹⁷Then the high priest took action; he and all who were with him (that is, the sect of the Sadducees), being filled with jealousy, ¹⁸arrested the apostles and put them in the public prison. ¹⁹But during the night an angel of the Lord opened the prison doors, brought them out, and said, ²⁰"Go, stand in the temple and tell the people the whole message about this life." ²¹When they heard this, they entered the temple at daybreak and went on with their teaching.

When the high priest and those with him arrived, they called together the council and the whole body of the elders of Israel, and sent to the prison to have them brought. ²²But when the temple police went there, they did not find them in the prison; so they returned and reported, ²³"We found the prison securely locked and the guards standing at the doors, but when we opened them, we found no one inside." ²⁴Now when the captain of the temple and the chief priests heard these words, they were perplexed about them, wondering what might be going on. [25]Then someone arrived and announced, "Look, the men whom you put in prison are standing in the temple and teaching the people!"

[26]Then the captain went with the temple police and brought them, but without violence, for they were afraid of being stoned by the people.

Reflection

We are so steeped in modern medical science that many are embarrassed by the almost magical healings presented in this passage. Look again. Luke alerts us to something much more significant: the fulfillment of the promised kingdom (as expressed in Isaiah 42, for instance.) The apostles are growing into Jesus' mission. Recall the opening of Jesus' public ministry:

> "The Spirit of the Lord is upon me, because he has anointed me to bring good news to the poor. He has sent me to proclaim release to the captives and recovery of sight to the blind, to let the oppressed go free" (Luke 4:18; see also Isaiah 61).

These passages are talking about more than physical healing. The sick are being restored economically so they can work, reenter society as whole people, and worship again in the temple. Community is being built as well as individuals being healed. Even the prisoners are being set free. This is divine work of restoring all things in Christ. The apostles are not the source of this power but agents—ministers—of reconciliation, continuing Jesus' work.

In Acts, healing is ordinary, not flashy or for profit: no public spectacles, no prior profession of faith, only a profession of need. There is no mandatory church attendance or a course before being healed. Healing comes first. It is grace. Some, like one of the ten healed lepers, follow the Way; some don't, but all are changed by their encounter with the life-giving God through the apostles' ministry. The apostles proclaim "the whole message of this life" (Acts 5:20). As Luke writes in chapter 4, "Today this scripture has been fulfilled in your hearing."

The Most Rev. Colin R. Johnson
Archbishop of Toronto and of Moosonee
Ontario, Canada

Questions _____

Where in your own life do you need Christ to heal or liberate you?

As a disciple of Christ, how are you an agent of healing and reconciliation in your community?

Prayer _____

God of healing and liberty, free us from all that binds and constricts us from fullness of life. Open our hearts to the needs around us that we may be faithful ministers of your healing presence in our midst. We ask this in the name of Jesus Christ. *Amen.*

Acts 5:27-42

²⁷When they had brought them, they had them stand before the council. The high priest questioned them, ²⁸saying, "We gave you strict orders not to teach in this name, yet here you have filled Jerusalem with your teaching and you are determined to bring this man's blood on us." ²⁹But Peter and the apostles answered, "We must obey God rather than any human authority. ³⁰The God of our ancestors raised up Jesus, whom you had killed by hanging him on a tree. ³¹God exalted him at his right hand as Leader and Savior that he might give repentance to Israel and forgiveness of sins. ³²And we are witnesses to these things, and so is the Holy Spirit whom God has given to those who obey him."

³³When they heard this, they were enraged and wanted to kill them. ³⁴But a Pharisee in the council named Gamaliel, a teacher of the law, respected by all the people, stood up and ordered the men to be put outside for a short time. ³⁵Then he said to them, "Fellow Israelites, consider carefully what you propose to do to these men. ³⁶For some time ago Theudas rose up, claiming to be somebody, and a number of men, about four hundred, joined him; but he was killed, and all who followed him were dispersed and disappeared. ³⁷After him Judas the Galilean rose up at the time of the census and got people to follow him; he also perished, and all who followed him were scattered. ³⁸So in the present case, I tell you, keep away from these men and let them alone; because if this plan or this undertaking is of human origin, it will fail; ³⁹but if it is of God, you will not be able to overthrow them—in that case you may even be found fighting against God!"

They were convinced by him, ⁴⁰and when they had called in the apostles, they had them flogged. Then they ordered them not to speak in the name of Jesus, and let them go. ⁴¹As they left the council, they rejoiced that they were considered worthy to suffer dishonor for the sake of the name. ⁴²And every day in the temple and at home they did not cease to teach and proclaim Jesus as the Messiah.

Reflection

Something has changed. Just a couple of months before, Peter and the disciples were in the Upper Room behind locked doors, desolate about what had just happened to Jesus and terrified of the authorities. In today's reading, they stand before those same authorities with confidence and conviction that brooks no fear. Fear, in fact, is the motivation of the authorities who do not know how to contain this new movement or what it will lead to. They know, for certain, that it will be a challenge to their power. Easter, Ascension, and Pentecost have changed everything.

The apostles' confidence is not the arrogant dismissal of all authority but their own; they are under the authority of the Holy Spirit, who generously calls forth life. They are brought before the council not only because they are teaching about Jesus but also because they are enacting his mission—healing and reconciling, putting compassionate reality to the words they speak that change people's lives. They accept the consequences, including suffering, for their actions "and rejoiced that they were considered worthy to suffer dishonor for the sake of the name [of Jesus]." The empowering of the Holy Spirit does not give protection but gives courage and faithfulness in the face of adversity. And at the end of the passage, another gift of the Spirit is named: joy, which is often a surprise in such circumstances.

The Most Rev. Colin R. Johnson
Archbishop of Toronto and of Moosonee
Ontario, Canada

Questions

How do we discern whether an action is simply defiance of authority or an act of courageous obedience in response to the call of the Spirit?

Do you find joy in the work and ministry that you are engaged in? How do you show it?

Prayer

Life-giving God, in the clamor of the many voices that call for our attention, give us attentive hearts and listening ears that we may hear your word addressed to us this day, wisdom to discern it, and courage to follow it, so that we may always rejoice in your loving service, through Jesus Christ our Lord. *Amen.*

Acts 6:1-7

6 Now during those days, when the disciples were increasing in number, the Hellenists complained against the Hebrews because their widows were being neglected in the daily distribution of food. ²And the twelve called together the whole community of the disciples and said, "It is not right that we should neglect the word of God in order to wait on tables. ³Therefore, friends, select from among yourselves seven men of good standing, full of the Spirit and of wisdom, whom we may appoint to this task, ⁴while we, for our part, will devote ourselves to prayer and to serving the word." ⁵What they said pleased the whole community, and they chose Stephen, a man full of faith and the Holy Spirit, together with Philip, Prochorus, Nicanor, Timon, Parmenas, and Nicolaus, a proselyte of Antioch. ⁶They had these men stand before the apostles, who prayed and laid their hands on them. ⁷The word of God continued to spread; the number of the disciples increased greatly in Jerusalem, and a great many of the priests became obedient to the faith.

Reflection

The earliest Jesus followers felt called to embody the highest ideals of love and mutual support across the cultural and racial divides of their time. Yet, like us, they were not immune to prejudice and misuse of power. So it was that the most vulnerable among the Hellenist (Greek-speaking) Christians were being discriminated against by the more powerful Hebrew Christians who controlled the community's food distribution.

The leadership's response to the Hellenists' complaint is instructive in several ways: First, they gathered the entire community together to address the situation. Second, they called for the raising up of new leaders from the ones who felt the sting of discrimination and were underrepresented in the church's authority structure. Third, they realized that in order for the community to flourish and grow, the structure needed to adapt to changing realities. They established a new division of work according to each person's gifts.

At first reading, it seems as though the Twelve felt that "waiting tables" was beneath them, a distraction from their higher calling to proclaim the word of God. But upon close examination, I sense a recognition that we all do our best work when we know what we do best—and get out of the way so others can do the same. When we do, the Spirit has more to work with, in and through us all, and the community flourishes.

The Rt. Rev. Mariann Edgar Budde
IX Bishop of the Diocese of Washington
District of Columbia

Questions _____

Where do you see or experience a power imbalance in your faith community or work/home environment?

How might God be calling you to offer your gifts and make room for others to do the same?

Prayer _____

Gracious God, you have called us to the highest ideals of love and community, yet in our sinfulness we fall short of that ideal. Thank you for those whose voices call us to accountability and give us courage to create the beloved community in which all are equally prized. Help us to identify and claim our gifts, and encourage others to do the same. In Christ we pray. *Amen.*

Acts 6:8-15

8Stephen, full of grace and power, did great wonders and signs among the people. 9Then some of those who belonged to the synagogue of the Freedmen (as it was called), Cyrenians, Alexandrians, and others of those from Cilicia and Asia, stood up and argued with Stephen. 10But they could not withstand the wisdom and the Spirit with which he spoke. 11Then they secretly instigated some men to say, "We have heard him speak blasphemous words against Moses and God." 12They stirred up the people as well as the elders and the scribes; then they suddenly confronted him, seized him, and brought him before the council. 13They set up false witnesses who said, "This man never stops saying things against this holy place and the law; 14for we have heard him say that this Jesus of Nazareth will destroy this place and will change the customs that Moses handed on to us." 15And all who sat in the council looked intently at him, and they saw that his face was like the face of an angel.

Reflection

Stephen was by all accounts an extraordinary man, and in Acts 6-8, he takes center stage. What we first learn of him is that he was "full of grace and power." In other words, he had experienced God's unconditional love for himself. He had encountered the living Christ. He had a clear sense of vocation that propelled him to serve others in Jesus' name and to engage in public discourse with his fellow Jews. And others saw in him the love of Jesus.

We don't know what caused those who belonged to the synagogue of the Freedmen to incite others to speak falsely against Stephen, but conflict and strife were in the air. The image before us today is of Stephen, seized by those who took issue with his teachings and forcibly brought before the council of the synagogue.

Imagine yourself in Stephen's place, seated before the highest religious authorities, surrounded by those who wish you harm. How does the grace and power of God sustain you in such times?

This is the great mystery of faith. It wasn't Stephen's power that enabled him to remain calm and steady under such tremendous pressure but rather the power of God at work in him. It wasn't his own grace but the grace and mercy of Christ that allowed him to remain compassionate toward those who had turned against him. When we experience such grace and power at work in us, we can only give glory to God, for God alone enables us to accomplish, as Paul writes, "far more than we can ask for or imagine."

The Rt. Rev. Mariann Edgar Budde
IX Bishop of the Diocese of Washington
District of Columbia

Questions _____

Recall a time when you felt sustained by a power greater than your own that enabled you to act or speak with more courage than you had. What does that experience tell you about God's grace and power at work in you?

How is the Holy Spirit inviting you to trust in God's grace and power where you are right now?

Prayer _____

Thank you, Jesus, for loving us unconditionally and allowing your grace and power to flow through us. Help us to trust that grace, to lean into your love and power in our times of need, so that we might love as you love, even when the cost is high. *Amen.*

Acts 7:1-60

7 Then the high priest asked him, "Are these things so?" ²And Stephen replied:

"Brothers and fathers, listen to me. The God of glory appeared to our ancestor Abraham when he was in Mesopotamia, before he lived in Haran, ³and said to him, 'Leave your country and your relatives and go to the land that I will show you.' ⁴Then he left the country of the Chaldeans and settled in Haran. After his father died, God had him move from there to this country in which you are now living. ⁵He did not give him any of it as a heritage, not even a foot's length, but promised to give it to him as his possession and to his descendants after him, even though he had no child. ⁶And God spoke in these terms, that his descendants would be resident aliens in a country belonging to others, who would enslave them and mistreat them during four hundred years.⁷'But I will judge the nation that they serve,' said God, 'and after that they shall come out and worship me in this place.' ⁸Then he gave him the covenant of circumcision. And so Abraham became the father of Isaac and circumcised him on the eighth day; and Isaac became the father of Jacob, and Jacob of the twelve patriarchs.

⁹"The patriarchs, jealous of Joseph, sold him into Egypt; but God was with him, ¹⁰and rescued him from all his afflictions, and enabled him to win favor and to show wisdom when he stood before Pharaoh, king of Egypt, who appointed him ruler over Egypt and over all his household. ¹¹Now there came a famine throughout Egypt and Canaan, and great suffering, and our ancestors could find no food. ¹²But when Jacob heard

that there was grain in Egypt, he sent our ancestors there on their first visit. ¹³On the second visit Joseph made himself known to his brothers, and Joseph's family became known to Pharaoh. ¹⁴Then Joseph sent and invited his father Jacob and all his relatives to come to him, seventy-five in all; ¹⁵so Jacob went down to Egypt. He himself died there as well as our ancestors, ¹⁶and their bodies were brought back to Shechem and laid in the tomb that Abraham had bought for a sum of silver from the sons of Hamor in Shechem.

¹⁷"But as the time drew near for the fulfillment of the promise that God had made to Abraham, our people in Egypt increased and multiplied ¹⁸until another king who had not known Joseph ruled over Egypt. ¹⁹He dealt craftily with our race and forced our ancestors to abandon their infants so that they would die. ²⁰At this time Moses was born, and he was beautiful before God. For three months he was brought up in his father's house; ²¹and when he was abandoned, Pharaoh's daughter adopted him and brought him up as her own son. ²²So Moses was instructed in all the wisdom of the Egyptians and was powerful in his words and deeds.

²³"When he was forty years old, it came into his heart to visit his relatives, the Israelites. ²⁴When he saw one of them being wronged, he defended the oppressed man and avenged him by striking down the Egyptian. ²⁵He supposed that his kinsfolk would understand that God through him was rescuing them, but they did not understand. ²⁶The next day he came to some of them as they were quarreling and tried to reconcile them, saying, 'Men, you are brothers; why do you wrong each other?' ²⁷But the man who was wronging his neighbor pushed Moses aside, saying, 'Who made you a ruler and a judge over us? ²⁸Do you want to kill me as you killed the Egyptian yesterday?'

[29]When he heard this, Moses fled and became a resident alien in the land of Midian. There he became the father of two sons.

[30]"Now when forty years had passed, an angel appeared to him in the wilderness of Mount Sinai, in the flame of a burning bush. [31]When Moses saw it, he was amazed at the sight; and as he approached to look, there came the voice of the Lord: [32]'I am the God of your ancestors, the God of Abraham, Isaac, and Jacob.' Moses began to tremble and did not dare to look. [33]Then the Lord said to him, 'Take off the sandals from your feet, for the place where you are standing is holy ground. [34]I have surely seen the mistreatment of my people who are in Egypt and have heard their groaning, and I have come down to rescue them. Come now, I will send you to Egypt.'

[35]"It was this Moses whom they rejected when they said, 'Who made you a ruler and a judge?' and whom God now sent as both ruler and liberator through the angel who appeared to him in the bush. [36]He led them out, having performed wonders and signs in Egypt, at the Red Sea, and in the wilderness for forty years. [37]This is the Moses who said to the Israelites, 'God will raise up a prophet for you from your own people as he raised me up.' [38]He is the one who was in the congregation in the wilderness with the angel who spoke to him at Mount Sinai, and with our ancestors; and he received living oracles to give to us. [39]Our ancestors were unwilling to obey him; instead, they pushed him aside, and in their hearts they turned back to Egypt, [40]saying to Aaron, 'Make gods for us who will lead the way for us; as for this Moses who led us out from the land of Egypt, we do not know what has happened to him.' [41]At that time they made a calf, offered a sacrifice to the idol, and reveled in the works of their hands. [42]But God turned away from them and

handed them over to worship the host of heaven, as it is written in the book of the prophets:

'Did you offer to me slain
victims and sacrifices
forty years in the
wilderness, O house
of Israel?
⁴³No; you took along the
tent of Moloch,
and the star of your god
Rephan,
the images that you
made to worship;
so I will remove you beyond
Babylon.'

⁴⁴"Our ancestors had the tent of testimony in the wilderness, as God directed when he spoke to Moses, ordering him to make it according to the pattern he had seen. ⁴⁵Our ancestors in turn brought it in with Joshua when they dispossessed the nations that God drove out before our ancestors. And it was there until the time of David, ⁴⁶who found favor with God and asked that he might find a dwelling place for the house of Jacob. ⁴⁷But it was Solomon who built a house for him. ⁴⁸Yet the Most High does not dwell in houses made with human hands; as the prophet says,

⁴⁹'Heaven is my throne,
and the earth is my
footstool.
What kind of house will
you build for me,
says the Lord,
or what is the place of my
rest?
⁵⁰Did not my hand make
all these things?'

⁵¹"You stiff-necked people, uncircumcised in heart and ears, you are forever opposing the Holy Spirit, just as your ancestors used to do. ⁵²Which of the prophets did your ancestors not persecute? They killed those who foretold the coming of the Righteous One, and now you have become his betrayers and murderers. ⁵³You are the ones that received the law as ordained by angels, and yet you have not kept it."

⁵⁴When they heard these things, they became enraged and ground

their teeth at Stephen. ⁵⁵But filled with the Holy Spirit, he gazed into heaven and saw the glory of God and Jesus standing at the right hand of God. ⁵⁶"Look," he said, "I see the heavens opened and the Son of Man standing at the right hand of God!" ⁵⁷But they covered their ears, and with a loud shout all rushed together against him. ⁵⁸Then they dragged him out of the city and began to stone him; and the witnesses laid their coats at the feet of a young man named Saul. ⁵⁹While they were stoning Stephen, he prayed, "Lord Jesus, receive my spirit." ⁶⁰Then he knelt down and cried out in a loud voice, "Lord, do not hold this sin against them." When he had said this, he died.

Reflection

Years after Stephen's martyrdom, Peter wrote to another group of Christians suffering persecution, "Always be ready to make your defense to anyone who demands from you an accounting for the hope that is in you" (1 Peter 3:15). I imagine Peter had the events of this passage in mind. Asked to defend himself against charges of blasphemy, Stephen gives an account of his faith that shows the history of salvation is written on his heart.

The comprehensiveness of Stephen's testimony reveals a faith grounded in intimacy with the stories of scripture, to the point that he recognizes them as his own. Stephen constantly locates both himself and his audience in the story. He uses the phrase "our ancestors" as a reminder of the direct link between his listeners and the figures of history.

In her book *Midrash: Reading the Bible with Question Marks* (Paraclete Press, 2007), Rabbi Sandy Eisenberg Sasso writes that God's intention for scripture "was for each generation to read its story into the text." Stephen's faith is built on an understanding of himself in relationship to scripture, and in his challenge to the council, he urges his accusers to do the same.

Stephen's speech does nothing to save his skin. He becomes the church's first martyr. But among those who heard him was Saul of Tarsus. Even as "Saul approved of their killing him," Stephen's testimony may have been preparing Saul's heart for the life-changing encounter with Jesus soon to come.

Brendan O'Sullivan-Hale
Canon to the Ordinary for Administration and Evangelism,
Diocese of Indianapolis
Indianapolis, Indiana

Questions

Is there a passage of the Bible you know so well it is part of your own story? How might you use that story to explain your faith to others?

How do you read your generation's story into chapter 7 of Acts?

Prayer

O God who caused all scripture to be written for our benefit, so graft its words into our hearts that through us, your prophets and apostles may speak even today to reveal Jesus Christ as your incarnate Word and the salvation of the world. *Amen.*

Acts 8:1-8

8 And Saul approved of their killing him.

That day a severe persecution began against the church in Jerusalem, and all except the apostles were scattered throughout the countryside of Judea and Samaria. ²Devout men buried Stephen and made loud lamentation over him. ³But Saul was ravaging the church by entering house after house; dragging off both men and women, he committed them to prison.

⁴Now those who were scattered went from place to place, proclaiming the word. ⁵Philip went down to the city of Samaria and proclaimed the Messiah to them. ⁶The crowds with one accord listened eagerly to what was said by Philip, hearing and seeing the signs that he did, ⁷for unclean spirits, crying with loud shrieks, came out of many who were possessed; and many others who were paralyzed or lame were cured. ⁸So there was great joy in that city.

Reflection

Just before his ascension, Jesus told the disciples that upon receiving the Holy Spirit, they "will be my witnesses in...Samaria, and to the ends of the earth." This is how the gospel came to Samaria: After the martyrdom of Stephen, Saul went from house to house, jailing believers, and all but the apostles fled Jerusalem. One of those who scattered, Philip, preached and performed miracles in a city in Samaria, bringing "great joy" to that city.

The healing and joy whose wellspring was the wreckage of the church in Jerusalem and Philip's flight to Samaria illustrates resurrection as the pattern for God's activity on earth—or at least it seems to. The risen Jesus is the same Jesus who died. Is it really resurrection if one dies and another lives?

We err when we attempt to assign meaning to the suffering of others. Doing so can quickly become failure in our responsibility to alleviate suffering or to offer the empty platitudes of "Everything happens for a reason," or "It's part of God's plan," when comforting those in grief.

Philip's success in Samaria cannot redeem Stephen's suffering and cannot unmake the sorrow of Stephen's friends. Yet Philip and Stephen shared a common purpose to bring people to wholeness in the love of Jesus Christ, and that purpose lives even today. The power of the resurrection strengthened Philip's heart to bring the joy of his faith to those who needed it, even in the face of Stephen's death, Saul's persecution, and his own fear. May our hearts be opened to receive the same strength in our own day.

Brendan O'Sullivan-Hale

Canon to the Ordinary for Administration and Evangelism,
Diocese of Indianapolis
Indianapolis, Indiana

Questions

Think of a struggle that you or a community you are part of have gone through. Where has new life come from in that struggle?

What happened to bring about that new life?

Prayer

O God who strengthens weak hands and fearful hearts, pour into us the same power that quickened Jesus' pulse in the tomb, that even amid failure, sorrow, and fear we may be bearers of your wholeness, healing, and joy. *Amen.*

Day 17

Acts 8:9-25

⁹Now a certain man named Simon had previously practiced magic in the city and amazed the people of Samaria, saying that he was someone great. ¹⁰All of them, from the least to the greatest, listened to him eagerly, saying, "This man is the power of God that is called Great." ¹¹And they listened eagerly to him because for a long time he had amazed them with his magic. ¹²But when they believed Philip, who was proclaiming the good news about the kingdom of God and the name of Jesus Christ, they were baptized, both men and women. ¹³Even Simon himself believed. After being baptized, he stayed constantly with Philip and was amazed when he saw the signs and great miracles that took place.

¹⁴Now when the apostles at Jerusalem heard that Samaria had accepted the word of God, they sent Peter and John to them. ¹⁵The two went down and prayed for them that they might receive the Holy Spirit ¹⁶(for as yet the Spirit had not come upon any of them; they had only been baptized in the name of the Lord Jesus). ¹⁷Then Peter and John laid their hands on them, and they received the Holy Spirit. ¹⁸Now when Simon saw that the Spirit was given through the laying on of the apostles' hands, he offered them money, ¹⁹saying, "Give me also this power so that anyone on whom I lay my hands may receive the Holy Spirit." ²⁰But Peter said to him, "May your silver perish with you, because you thought you could obtain God's gift with money! ²¹You have no part or share in this, for your heart is not right before God. ²²Repent therefore of this wickedness of yours, and pray to the Lord that, if possible, the intent of your

heart may be forgiven you. ²³For I see that you are in the gall of bitterness and the chains of wickedness." ²⁴Simon answered, "Pray for me to the Lord, that nothing of what you have said may happen to me."

²⁵Now after Peter and John had testified and spoken the word of the Lord, they returned to Jerusalem, proclaiming the good news to many villages of the Samaritans.

Reflection

Humanity has always misunderstood the concept of a free gift from God. From the earliest times, we have sought to wrestle the stuff of heaven into a more comfortable economy, into systems we know how to navigate and manipulate with the resources we have on hand. This tendency to treat grace as though it can be exchanged like property or favors has played a notorious role in church history. Simon, our misguided new Christian in today's passage, becomes the namesake for the sin of simony—that is, buying or selling ecclesiastical privileges such as asking people to pay money in exchange for laying on of hands to receive the Holy Spirit.

Simony has been prominent in the historical relationship between church and state. Because of this sordid past, we tend to think of simony as an institutional problem, involving popes and bishops and money-grubbing priests. But I wonder if thinking in this way might keep us feeling inoculated from something that's a much more present danger to the welfare of our souls.

In our passage today, Peter rebukes Simon and denies him a share in the apostolic ministry because Simon intends to "obtain God's gift with money." The story doesn't say Simon intends to benefit personally from the gift. He may very well have wanted to serve God. Where Simon has gone wrong is in assuming that God operates in the terms of the world, that God's way of being is subject to human systems of value and meaning. Simon's mistake, while perhaps not self-serving, nevertheless exhibits a profound misunderstanding of the Divine.

Grace is truly a gift. It flows from the upside-down, inside-out kingdom of heaven to challenge our most basic assumptions and subvert our most comfortable economies.

The Rev. Chad Sundin, osbc

Chaplain for Episcopal Campus Ministries, Arizona State University
Vicar, St. Augustine's Episcopal Parish
Tempe, Arizona

Questions _____

What is your most comfortable economy, and how have you used its resources to try to obtain something from God?

Which of your assumptions might need some adjusting so that you can better understand how God operates?

Prayer _____

Holy One, thank you for your gift of grace that is truly a gift. May we learn to relate to you not on our terms, but on your terms, receiving without payment what flows from your generous hands. In the name of Jesus. *Amen.*

Acts 8:26-40

²⁶Then an angel of the Lord said to Philip, "Get up and go toward the south to the road that goes down from Jerusalem to Gaza." (This is a wilderness road.) ²⁷So he got up and went. Now there was an Ethiopian eunuch, a court official of the Candace, queen of the Ethiopians, in charge of her entire treasury. He had come to Jerusalem to worship ²⁸and was returning home; seated in his chariot, he was reading the prophet Isaiah. ²⁹Then the Spirit said to Philip, "Go over to this chariot and join it." ³⁰So Philip ran up to it and heard him reading the prophet Isaiah. He asked, "Do you understand what you are reading?" ³¹He replied, "How can I, unless someone guides me?" And he invited Philip to get in and sit beside him. ³²Now the passage of the scripture that he was reading was this:

"Like a sheep he was led
　　to the slaughter,
and like a lamb silent
　　before its shearer,
　so he does not open his
　　mouth.
³³In his humiliation justice
　　was denied him.
　Who can describe his
　　generation?
For his life is taken away
　　from the earth."

³⁴The eunuch asked Philip, "About whom, may I ask you, does the prophet say this, about himself or about someone else?" ³⁵Then Philip began to speak, and starting with this scripture, he proclaimed to him the good news about Jesus. ³⁶As they were going along the road, they came to some water; and the eunuch said, "Look, here is water! What is to prevent me from being baptized?" ³⁸He commanded the chariot to stop, and both of them, Philip and the eunuch,

went down into the water, and Philip baptized him. [39]When they came up out of the water, the Spirit of the Lord snatched Philip away; the eunuch saw him no more, and went on his way rejoicing. [40]But Philip found himself at Azotus, and as he was passing through the region, he proclaimed the good news to all the towns until he came to Caesarea.

Reflection

In the remote wilderness of the Judean desert sits the traditional site where John the Baptist baptized Jesus in the Jordan River. In early 2016, I visited this site and encountered a large group of Ethiopian Orthodox Christians. Some were celebrating mass in true Coptic fashion, with incense, elaborate vestments, golden torches, and tall crosses. Others were down on the banks or waist-deep in the river wearing sheer white robes in order to be baptized or to renew their baptismal vows in the slow, muddy water. On that late January day, I had come upon an Ethiopian Orthodox observance of Epiphany called "Timkat." Hundreds of pilgrims had made their way by bus from the Horn of Africa to celebrate this great feast at the Jordan.

Today's story from Acts includes an entourage of Ethiopian pilgrims traveling in the opposite direction on approximately the same road taken by the pilgrims I encountered. I wonder if it was the Jordan about which the first-century Ethiopian eunuch exclaimed, "Look, here is water! What is to prevent me from being baptized?" By receiving baptism in the Judean wilderness, this official in the ancient Ethiopian court forged the beginnings of what is today an unbroken line between the apostles and the Ethiopian Church.

But no matter the longevity of our connection to the waters of baptism, every Christian must return with the heart of a pilgrim to the truth of their identity: God has moved in and around each of our lives such that we have heard the good news about Jesus and found our welcome into God's family.

The Rev. Chad Sundin, osbc
Chaplain for Episcopal Campus Ministries, Arizona State University
Vicar, St. Augustine's Episcopal Parish
Tempe, Arizona

Questions

Reflect upon your journey of faith. Where do you see God's movement leading you into your encounter with Christ?

Is there anything that you feel prevents you from receiving the gift of your place in God's family?

Prayer

Kind and generous God, give us eyes to see your hand guiding us toward our true home as full members of your one family, spanning time and space. May our experience of your welcome inspire us to extend an unreserved welcome to all who seek a deeper knowledge of you; through Jesus Christ our Lord. *Amen.*

Acts 9:1-31

9 Meanwhile Saul, still breathing threats and murder against the disciples of the Lord, went to the high priest ²and asked him for letters to the synagogues at Damascus, so that if he found any who belonged to the Way, men or women, he might bring them bound to Jerusalem. ³Now as he was going along and approaching Damascus, suddenly a light from heaven flashed around him. ⁴He fell to the ground and heard a voice saying to him, "Saul, Saul, why do you persecute me?" ⁵He asked, "Who are you, Lord?" The reply came, "I am Jesus, whom you are persecuting. ⁶But get up and enter the city, and you will be told what you are to do." ⁷The men who were traveling with him stood speechless because they heard the voice but saw no one. ⁸Saul got up from the ground, and though his eyes were open, he could see nothing; so they led him by the hand and brought him into Damascus. ⁹For three days he was without sight, and neither ate nor drank.

¹⁰Now there was a disciple in Damascus named Ananias. The Lord said to him in a vision, "Ananias." He answered, "Here I am, Lord." ¹¹The Lord said to him, "Get up and go to the street called Straight, and at the house of Judas look for a man of Tarsus named Saul. At this moment he is praying, ¹²and he has seen in a vision a man named Ananias come in and lay his hands on him so that he might regain his sight." ¹³But Ananias answered, "Lord, I have heard from many about this man, how much evil he has done to your saints in Jerusalem; ¹⁴and here he has authority from the chief priests to bind all who invoke your name." ¹⁵But the Lord said to him, "Go, for he is an instrument

whom I have chosen to bring my name before Gentiles and kings and before the people of Israel; [16]I myself will show him how much he must suffer for the sake of my name." [17]So Ananias went and entered the house. He laid his hands on Saul and said, "Brother Saul, the Lord Jesus, who appeared to you on your way here, has sent me so that you may regain your sight and be filled with the Holy Spirit." [18]And immediately something like scales fell from his eyes, and his sight was restored. Then he got up and was baptized, [19]and after taking some food, he regained his strength.

For several days he was with the disciples in Damascus, [20]and immediately he began to proclaim Jesus in the synagogues, saying, "He is the Son of God." [21]All who heard him were amazed and said, "Is not this the man who made havoc in Jerusalem among those who invoked this name? And has he not come here for the purpose of bringing them bound before the chief priests?" [22]Saul became increasingly more powerful and confounded the Jews who lived in Damascus by proving that Jesus was the Messiah.

[23]After some time had passed, the Jews plotted to kill him, [24]but their plot became known to Saul. They were watching the gates day and night so that they might kill him; [25]but his disciples took him by night and let him down through an opening in the wall, lowering him in a basket.

[26]When he had come to Jerusalem, he attempted to join the disciples; and they were all afraid of him, for they did not believe that he was a disciple. [27]But Barnabas took him, brought him to the apostles, and described for them how on the road he had seen the Lord, who had spoken to him, and how in Damascus he had spoken boldly in the name of Jesus. [28]So he went in and out among them in Jerusalem, speaking boldly in the name of the Lord. [29]He spoke and argued with the Hellenists;

Reflection

Before being ordained, I spent a summer teaching in a seminary in Kenya. One day, each of my students told me the exact date and time of their conversion. In each case, the students recounted a dramatic moment in which they abandoned a previous life and began a new life in Christ.

For many mainline Christians, this is a highly unusual experience. For evangelicals, however, Paul's "Damascus Road" experience is a model for Christian transformation. Paul was struck blind. His old life abruptly ended. He turned around 180 degrees. Strangers befriended him despite his past abhorrent behavior as a zealous Christian persecutor.

John Newton, the eighteenth-century author of "Amazing Grace," had a similar experience. He was a militant atheist, bully, and blasphemer, who was press-ganged into the navy at the age of eighteen. Newton recklessly broke the rules and was publicly flogged for desertion. He was hated and feared by his crewmates and became a slave trader.

On March 10, 1748, when Newton was twenty-three, his ship encountered a severe storm off the coast of Donegal and nearly sank. Newton cried out to God as the ship filled with water. God rescued him, and Newton began a new life with God. Newton prayed and read the Bible each day and later joined William Wilberforce as a leader in the campaign to abolish the slave trade. Newton penned his famous hymn, writing:

> Amazing grace! How sweet the sound
> That saved a wretch like me!
> I once was lost but now I'm found,
> Was blind, but now I see.

Like Paul, Newton's blind eyes were opened. Christian writer Max Lucado notes, "God loves you just the way you are, but he [doesn't intend] to leave you that way." Conversion suggests that God is never done with any of us, for we are clay in the Potter's hands.

The Rev. Marek P. Zabriskie
Rector, St. Thomas' Episcopal Church, Whitemarsh
Founder of **The Bible Challenge**
Fort Washington, Pennsylvania

Questions

Have you experienced gradual spiritual growth or do you have a defining moment in your life that abruptly changed you and drew you closer to God?

Were you previously blind in some ways, and has God helped you to see more clearly? Who befriended you on your Damascus Road?

Prayer

Gracious, holy, and life-giving God, we thank you for healing our blindness and bringing us to our knees by your graceful touch until we succumbed to your love and mercy. Help us to continue faithfully as your disciples, trusting that you are always transforming us so that we may see you more clearly and love you more dearly. *Amen.*

Acts 9:32-43

³²Now as Peter went here and there among all the believers, he came down also to the saints living in Lydda. ³³There he found a man named Aeneas, who had been bedridden for eight years, for he was paralyzed. ³⁴Peter said to him, "Aeneas, Jesus Christ heals you; get up and make your bed!" And immediately he got up. ³⁵And all the residents of Lydda and Sharon saw him and turned to the Lord.

³⁶Now in Joppa there was a disciple whose name was Tabitha, which in Greek is Dorcas. She was devoted to good works and acts of charity. ³⁷At that time she became ill and died. When they had washed her, they laid her in a room upstairs. ³⁸Since Lydda was near Joppa, the disciples, who heard that Peter was there, sent two men to him with the request, "Please come to us without delay." ³⁹So Peter got up and went with them; and when he arrived, they took him to the room upstairs. All the widows stood beside him, weeping and showing tunics and other clothing that Dorcas had made while she was with them. ⁴⁰Peter put all of them outside, and then he knelt down and prayed. He turned to the body and said, "Tabitha, get up." Then she opened her eyes, and seeing Peter, she sat up. ⁴¹He gave her his hand and helped her up. Then calling the saints and widows, he showed her to be alive. ⁴²This became known throughout Joppa, and many believed in the Lord. ⁴³Meanwhile he stayed in Joppa for some time with a certain Simon, a tanner.

Reflection

The summer that I lived in Africa, a missionary lent me a copy of Francis McNutt's book *Healing*. I was attending Yale Divinity School and proudly thought that such books were beneath my intellectual training. However, having no other books, I read it carefully.

I was astonished by the vast amount of healing that McNutt recounted as occurring in the New Testament, something that many biblical scholars glance over. Jesus constantly healed people in physical ways. Luke, the author of the gospel bearing his name and the Book of Acts, eloquently depicts Jesus' ability to heal.

In this passage, we see the gift of healing manifested in Peter's life. Peter made several missionary journeys to exhort and encourage the faithful of the early church. On a trip to Lydda, a town on the plain of Sharon some twenty-five miles northwest of Jerusalem, he healed Aeneas, a paralyzed man whose name means "praiseworthy."

Learning that Peter was only ten miles away, the disciples asked him to come to Joppa, an important Christian center. Dorcas, also known as Tabitha, had just died. She was known for her good works and acts of charity, including the making of tunics and other garments for the poor. Dorcas mirrored the praiseworthy woman of Proverbs 31:13, 20. She gave not only her coins, but herself to God. When she died, many mourned her.

Like Elisha who healed a child of the Shunammite woman, Peter knelt down, prayed over her, and said "Tabitha, get up." Her eyes opened, and Dorcas was filled with new life.

We may not have the power to raise the dead, but we have been called and given the power to open blind eyes. These two healings were some of the first miracles performed by an apostle, and they gained many believers.

The Rev. Marek P. Zabriskie
Rector, St. Thomas' Episcopal Church, Whitemarsh
Founder of The Bible Challenge
Fort Washington, Pennsylvania

Questions

How has God healed you and helped you to get up and move forward when you were stuck and paralyzed by life's circumstances?

Have you ever traveled intentionally as a Christian on pilgrimage or as part of a mission team?

Where do you see healing occurring in your church, family, workplace or community? Who would you list among the healers that you know?

Prayer

Almighty God, you alone have the power to free our paralyzed limbs when fear overcomes us and courage departs us. Help us to accept your graces and healing mercies so that we might rise with boldness and move forward from situations in which we are stuck and lack the ability to free ourselves. In Jesus' name we pray. *Amen.*

Acts 10:1-16

10 In Caesarea there was a man named Cornelius, a centurion of the Italian Cohort, as it was called. ²He was a devout man who feared God with all his household; he gave alms generously to the people and prayed constantly to God. ³One afternoon at about three o'clock he had a vision in which he clearly saw an angel of God coming in and saying to him, "Cornelius." ⁴He stared at him in terror and said, "What is it, Lord?" He answered, "Your prayers and your alms have ascended as a memorial before God. ⁵Now send men to Joppa for a certain Simon who is called Peter; ⁶he is lodging with Simon, a tanner, whose house is by the seaside." ⁷When the angel who spoke to him had left, he called two of his slaves and a devout soldier from the ranks of those who served him, ⁸and after telling them everything, he sent them to Joppa.

⁹About noon the next day, as they were on their journey and approaching the city, Peter went up on the roof to pray. ¹⁰He became hungry and wanted something to eat; and while it was being prepared, he fell into a trance. ¹¹He saw the heaven opened and something like a large sheet coming down, being lowered to the ground by its four corners. ¹²In it were all kinds of four-footed creatures and reptiles and birds of the air. ¹³Then he heard a voice saying, "Get up, Peter; kill and eat." ¹⁴But Peter said, "By no means, Lord; for I have never eaten anything that is profane or unclean." ¹⁵The voice said to him again, a second time, "What God has made clean, you must not call profane." ¹⁶This happened three times, and the thing was suddenly taken up to heaven.

Reflection

"What is it, Lord?"

How often do we ask this question about our faith, our journey, and our individual lives? The question could be a searching inquisition as to the next tentative steps in life. The question could be an exasperated declaration of frustration with a current life situation. Maybe this query is a hopeful expectation of hearing God's voice and the wonder found in Jesus Christ. "What is it, Lord?" transcends a simple sentence or response. It is a profound reflection of the depth of our relationship with God and how the Divine gives meaning to our lives.

Cornelius is a devout man and loves God. His openness to sacred listening is a fundamental recognition of the power of God in our lives: God who changes the Apostle Peter, God who redirects our simplistic understanding of what is clean and what is profane, God who seeks the continual conversation between Creator and creation.

Listen, look, and learn. God moves through each one of us. God is urging, prodding, and nudging—and in some instances, we may hear an exasperated declaration of frustration. The beauty of the relationship and the depth of intimacy with our Creator gives meaning. It changes our relationship with one another. With each step and prayer, we must respond like Cornelius: "What is it Lord?" The path may be unexpected and the destination unforeseen. We may and should ask the same question again and again. Ask the question, seek God's face, and then respond. God is always with us.

The Rt. Rev. Daniel G. P. Gutierrez
XVI Bishop of the Diocese of Pennsylvania
Philadelphia, Pennsylvania

Questions

In what instances have spiritual questions led you into deeper conversations with God?

Where has your questioning caused you to identify with someone like Cornelius or even Peter?

Prayers

O most holy One, open my heart and ears to your divine voice. Give me the questions so I can ask, "What is it, Lord?" Give me the eyes, heart, and strength to open my life to your everlasting presence. In the name of our Lord and Savior Jesus Christ. *Amen.*

Acts 10:17-33

¹⁷Now while Peter was greatly puzzled about what to make of the vision that he had seen, suddenly the men sent by Cornelius appeared. They were asking for Simon's house and were standing by the gate. ¹⁸They called out to ask whether Simon, who was called Peter, was staying there. ¹⁹While Peter was still thinking about the vision, the Spirit said to him, "Look, three men are searching for you. ²⁰Now get up, go down, and go with them without hesitation; for I have sent them." ²¹So Peter went down to the men and said, "I am the one you are looking for; what is the reason for your coming?" ²²They answered, "Cornelius, a centurion, an upright and God-fearing man, who is well spoken of by the whole Jewish nation, was directed by a holy angel to send for you to come to his house and to hear what you have to say." ²³So Peter invited them in and gave them lodging.

The next day he got up and went with them, and some of the believers from Joppa accompanied him. ²⁴The following day they came to Caesarea. Cornelius was expecting them and had called together his relatives and close friends. ²⁵On Peter's arrival Cornelius met him, and falling at his feet, worshiped him. ²⁶But Peter made him get up, saying, "Stand up; I am only a mortal." ²⁷And as he talked with him, he went in and found that many had assembled; ²⁸and he said to them, "You yourselves know that it is unlawful for a Jew to associate with or to visit a Gentile; but God has shown me that I should not call anyone profane or unclean. ²⁹So when I was sent for, I came without objection. Now may I ask why you sent for me?"

³⁰Cornelius replied, "Four days ago at this very hour, at three o'clock, I was praying in my house when suddenly a man in dazzling clothes stood before me. ³¹He said, 'Cornelius, your prayer has been heard and your alms have been remembered before God. ³²Send therefore to Joppa and ask for Simon, who is called Peter; he is staying in the home of Simon, a tanner, by the sea.' ³³Therefore I sent for you immediately, and you have been kind enough to come. So now all of us are here in the presence of God to listen to all that the Lord has commanded you to say."

Reflection

In the previous passage, the spirit of the Lord touches both Cornelius and Peter. It is not a gentle urging or silent prodding; the Lord is sending direct and explicit messages. God tells Cornelius: Do whatever it takes, get up. Go and find Peter!

In much the same way, the Spirit awakens and shakes Peter with the understanding that God is revealing the message in unexpected, new, and transformative ways. The interaction and discernment of the spirit is life-changing on multiple levels. We are led to the realization that the voice of God takes us to places that are unseen and, at times, unknown. Moreover, the voice of God can come in the form of those seeking a place of community (Cornelius gathering people, the three men carrying the message). Throughout time, we discover that God continually surprises, upends, and uplifts our being. Definite answers often lead to further questions, and the questions inevitably move us to deeper faith and trust in God. Once again, the relationship with God is what gives meaning.

It is also important to reflect on the responsiveness and faithfulness of Cornelius and Peter. Their willingness to listen to the spirit, despite the unknowing, begins to breathe the spirit of awakening into the growing church. Peter and Cornelius do not sit in worry and wonder. They act. They move and respond to the Lord. They might have more questions than answers. However, this does not lessen their faith or immobilize their faithfulness. In fact, Peter and Cornelius are emboldened. They get up and walk and seek out what the Lord has planned.

The Rt. Rev. Daniel G. P. Gutierrez
XVI Bishop of the Diocese of Pennsylvania
Philadelphia, Pennsylvania

Questions

What is holding the world back in this day and time from listening and then actively responding to the spirit of the Lord?

What steps can we take in our workplace, homes, and churches to overcome the obstacles?

Prayer

O most Holy One, you call us forth and direct our paths to bring your vision to the world. We are commanded by your words to listen. Give us a listening life and a hopeful heart to go forth among your people. All this we ask in the name of your life-giving Son Jesus Christ. *Amen.*

Acts 10:34-48

³⁴Then Peter began to speak to them: "I truly understand that God shows no partiality, ³⁵but in every nation anyone who fears him and does what is right is acceptable to him. ³⁶You know the message he sent to the people of Israel, preaching peace by Jesus Christ—he is Lord of all. ³⁷That message spread throughout Judea, beginning in Galilee after the baptism that John announced: ³⁸how God anointed Jesus of Nazareth with the Holy Spirit and with power; how he went about doing good and healing all who were oppressed by the devil, for God was with him. ³⁹We are witnesses to all that he did both in Judea and in Jerusalem. They put him to death by hanging him on a tree; ⁴⁰but God raised him on the third day and allowed him to appear, ⁴¹not to all the people but to us who were chosen by God as witnesses, and who ate and drank with him after he rose from the dead. ⁴²He commanded us to preach to the people and to testify that he is the one ordained by God as judge of the living and the dead. ⁴³All the prophets testify about him that everyone who believes in him receives forgiveness of sins through his name."

⁴⁴While Peter was still speaking, the Holy Spirit fell upon all who heard the word. ⁴⁵The circumcised believers who had come with Peter were astounded that the gift of the Holy Spirit had been poured out even on the Gentiles, ⁴⁶for they heard them speaking in tongues and extolling God. Then Peter said, ⁴⁷"Can anyone withhold the water for baptizing these people who have received the Holy Spirit just as we have?" ⁴⁸So he ordered them to be baptized in the name of Jesus Christ. Then they invited him to stay for several days.

Reflection

As a teenager, I often participated in spiritual retreats as part of my youth group experience. One of the songs that stands out in my mind is a popular tune by the southern quartet known as The Imperials entitled "You're the Only Jesus." The song's refrain tells us that today's Christians will be the "only Jesus" some will ever see. It is a song about the importance of witnessing and testimony.

When I read this passage from Acts, I am reminded of the great impact of Peter's testimony and how many embraced the good news of Jesus—and were open to accept baptism—because of it. Yet, Peter's personal testimony did more than simply retell the story; God effectively used Peter to open the hearts of early believers to the gift of the Holy Spirit.

I believe today's Christians must also be ready to witness to the gospel as Peter did. We must not be shy to share what we too have seen and heard and the many ways we have experienced the power of the Spirit in our lives. We cannot ignore that while people seem to be turned off by organized religion, they somehow appear to be hungry for God's Word. I find that oftentimes those of us who have grown up in the church and have an active personal relationship with Jesus are too slow to boldly share the gift which we have received. We need the courage of the apostles to share our testimony and to remind us that we may be indeed the only Jesus some will ever meet.

The Very Rev. Albert R. Cutié
Dean, Broward, Florida
Rector, St. Benedict's Episcopal Church
Plantation, Florida

Questions _____

What was the last time you shared what God has done in your life?

Do you find yourself able to speak freely about the weather, sports, news, or any other issue, but avoid speaking or witnessing about your faith in Jesus?

Prayer _____

Lord of the Good News, we profess and we believe that your church is apostolic—a people sent out. We pray that you send us out into the world and give us the courage to proclaim with joy and compassion the life-giving and transformative message of Jesus Christ. *Amen.*

Acts 11:1-18

11 Now the apostles and the believers who were in Judea heard that the Gentiles had also accepted the word of God. ²So when Peter went up to Jerusalem, the circumcised believers criticized him, ³saying, "Why did you go to uncircumcised men and eat with them?" ⁴Then Peter began to explain it to them, step by step, saying, ⁵"I was in the city of Joppa praying, and in a trance I saw a vision. There was something like a large sheet coming down from heaven, being lowered by its four corners; and it came close to me. ⁶As I looked at it closely I saw four-footed animals, beasts of prey, reptiles, and birds of the air. ⁷I also heard a voice saying to me, 'Get up, Peter; kill and eat.' ⁸But I replied, 'By no means, Lord; for nothing profane or unclean has ever entered my mouth.' ⁹But a second time the voice answered from heaven, 'What God has made clean, you must not call profane.' ¹⁰This happened three times; then everything was pulled up again to heaven. ¹¹At that very moment three men, sent to me from Caesarea, arrived at the house where we were. ¹²The Spirit told me to go with them and not to make a distinction between them and us. These six brothers also accompanied me, and we entered the man's house. ¹³He told us how he had seen the angel standing in his house and saying, 'Send to Joppa and bring Simon, who is called Peter; ¹⁴he will give you a message by which you and your entire household will be saved.' ¹⁵And as I began to speak, the Holy Spirit fell upon them just as it had upon us at the beginning. ¹⁶And I remembered the word of the Lord, how he had said, 'John baptized with water, but you will be baptized with the Holy Spirit.' ¹⁷If then God gave them the same gift that he gave

us when we believed in the Lord Jesus Christ, who was I that I could hinder God?" [18]When they heard this, they were silenced. And they praised God, saying, "Then God has given even to the Gentiles the repentance that leads to life."

Reflection

Who is "in" and who is "out"? As we see in this passage from Acts, it was not easy for some early Christian believers to readily embrace those who did not have the benefit of the faith, traditions, and background of the people of Israel. Only God's chosen people had received the Law and the Prophets. They were also the ones who longed for and lived in expectation of God's Messiah for generations. Yet, here is Peter spending time with, and even baptizing, Gentiles who were uncircumcised. To the circumcised believers, this represented a serious offense. Peter was mingling with those who were not card-carrying members of their club.

It's ironic how some things never change. I often hear longtime members of our church refer to themselves as cradle Episcopalians or cradle Anglicans with a sense of pride. Yet, I wonder how many of us realize that to follow Jesus, we must be Christians by choice. Being born into the church, being lifetime members, or even being baptized does not always translate into living a truly Christian life. We are truly "in" when we take the gospel seriously and live according to the message of God's love revealed in Jesus Christ.

Today's church seeks to be inclusive and has made a lot of progress to make good on the words "All are welcome." Yet we must re-examine ourselves to ensure that inclusion is not just a passing trend but truly a response to a gospel mandate. We must be inclusive and accepting of all because it is God's call to us. Because, ultimately, God's children must all be in.

The Very Rev. Albert R. Cutié
Dean, Broward, Florida
Rector, St. Benedict's Episcopal Church
Plantation, Florida

A Journey Through Acts

Questions

Can I identify specific moments when I, like the early believers who were circumcised, singled out people who did not share my heritage, background, or religious experience?

Am I aware that inclusion and my openness to all is part of fully living the commandment of love?

Prayer

God of love, free our hearts of every ideology or attitude that keeps us from loving and accepting all people as your beloved children. Help us to be instruments of peace and bridge builders for all, so that everyone may feel truly welcomed and at home in your church. *Amen.*

Acts 11:19-30

¹⁹Now those who were scattered because of the persecution that took place over Stephen traveled as far as Phoenicia, Cyprus, and Antioch, and they spoke the word to no one except Jews. ²⁰But among them were some men of Cyprus and Cyrene who, on coming to Antioch, spoke to the Hellenists also, proclaiming the Lord Jesus. ²¹The hand of the Lord was with them, and a great number became believers and turned to the Lord. ²²News of this came to the ears of the church in Jerusalem, and they sent Barnabas to Antioch. ²³When he came and saw the grace of God, he rejoiced, and he exhorted them all to remain faithful to the Lord with steadfast devotion; ²⁴for he was a good man, full of the Holy Spirit and of faith. And a great many people were brought to the Lord.

²⁵Then Barnabas went to Tarsus to look for Saul, ²⁶and when he had found him, he brought him to Antioch. So it was that for an entire year they met with the church and taught a great many people, and it was in Antioch that the disciples were first called "Christians."

²⁷At that time prophets came down from Jerusalem to Antioch. ²⁸One of them named Agabus stood up and predicted by the Spirit that there would be a severe famine over all the world; and this took place during the reign of Claudius. ²⁹The disciples determined that according to their ability, each would send relief to the believers living in Judea; ³⁰this they did, sending it to the elders by Barnabas and Saul.

Reflection

"It was in Antioch that the disciples were first called 'Christians.'"

I can't imagine that the word "Christian" was meant as a compliment outside the community of believers in Antioch, The Romans probably didn't use the word to describe someone like Barnabas, "a good man, full of…faith." The label "Christian" probably meant *those* people, the ones who did strange things like sending money to people in another city just because they needed help.

As much as I love Jesus, sometimes it is hard for me to accept the badge of Christian as a compliment. I see our church at war with itself, expending precious energy on minutia instead of focusing on loving our neighbors. I see our church turning a blind eye to the oppression it has perpetrated over centuries, neglecting to repair the damage it has caused. I see our church shaming nonbelievers, seekers, and others who are finding their way. I fear being labeled as one of *those* people.

Perhaps my best course of action is to listen to Barnabas's advice to the church in Antioch, to remain faithful to the Lord, with steadfast devotion. My purpose is not to fix the capital-C Church; neither is it to change people's minds about what a "Christian" does or is. My purpose is to follow Jesus faithfully, steadfastly, and devotedly.

Holli S. Powell, CPA
Lay Preacher
Host of **The Collect Call** *podcast*
Lexington, Kentucky

Questions

What do you think when you hear the word "Christian?" Does the word have positive or negative connotations?

Are you able to claim it for yourself?

Prayer

Merciful God, I am thankful that I do not have to be the poster child for Christianity. Help me to remember that my job is to love Jesus and to follow where God leads me. *Amen.*

A Journey Through Acts

Acts 12:1-19

12 About that time King Herod laid violent hands upon some who belonged to the church. ²He had James, the brother of John, killed with the sword. ³After he saw that it pleased the Jews, he proceeded to arrest Peter also. (This was during the festival of Unleavened Bread.) ⁴When he had seized him, he put him in prison and handed him over to four squads of soldiers to guard him, intending to bring him out to the people after the Passover. ⁵While Peter was kept in prison, the church prayed fervently to God for him.

⁶The very night before Herod was going to bring him out, Peter, bound with two chains, was sleeping between two soldiers, while guards in front of the door were keeping watch over the prison. ⁷Suddenly an angel of the Lord appeared and a light shone in the cell. He tapped Peter on the side and woke him, saying, "Get up quickly." And the chains fell off his wrists. ⁸The angel said to him, "Fasten your belt and put on your sandals." He did so. Then he said to him, "Wrap your cloak around you and follow me." ⁹Peter went out and followed him; he did not realize that what was happening with the angel's help was real; he thought he was seeing a vision. ¹⁰After they had passed the first and the second guard, they came before the iron gate leading into the city. It opened for them of its own accord, and they went outside and walked along a lane, when suddenly the angel left him. ¹¹Then Peter came to himself and said, "Now I am sure that the Lord has sent his angel and rescued me from the hands of Herod and from all that the Jewish people were expecting."

¹²As soon as he realized this, he went to the house of Mary, the mother of John whose other name was Mark, where many had gathered and were praying. ¹³When he knocked at the outer gate, a maid named Rhoda came to answer. ¹⁴On recognizing Peter's voice, she was so overjoyed that, instead of opening the gate, she ran in and announced that Peter was standing at the gate. ¹⁵They said to her, "You are out of your mind!" But she insisted that it was so. They said, "It is his angel." ¹⁶Meanwhile Peter continued knocking; and when they opened the gate, they saw him and were amazed. ¹⁷He motioned to them with his hand to be silent, and described for them how the Lord had brought him out of the prison. And he added, "Tell this to James and to the believers." Then he left and went to another place.

¹⁸When morning came, there was no small commotion among the soldiers over what had become of Peter. ¹⁹When Herod had searched for him and could not find him, he examined the guards and ordered them to be put to death. Then he went down from Judea to Caesarea and stayed there.

Reflection

When I first read this story, I felt uncomfortable. I thought about the faithful people I know, some of whom are battling cancer, some of whom have lost loved ones to divorce or estrangement or death, some of whom are worried about their finances and their jobs and their futures. I thought about all the prayers that are said—to heal them, to ease their suffering, to keep them safe. Then I thought about all the faithful people who I don't know around the world, all the pain in the world, and all the prayers for justice and healing and peace that are said. And still, people suffer. They stay sick. Injustice wins. Meanwhile, in this chapter of Acts, God executes a *Mission Impossible*-style rescue, maneuvering Peter out of prison in the dead of night past chains, soldiers, and guards. Why isn't God answering my prayers so dramatically?

But then I remember Mary's maid, Rhoda. Rhoda hears a knock at the gate and finds the literal answer to her prayers, her employer's prayers, the prayers of everyone gathered, standing there. And Rhoda turns and runs into the house, leaving Peter outside! Rhoda's emotions overtake her before she can accept what God has brought to her door.

I can't (and shouldn't) expect an action-movie answer to my prayers, but healing and grace and love and peace—the things I pray for myself and others—are all around me. In fact, answers to my prayers may be waiting just outside, if only I can compose myself long enough to invite them in.

Holli S. Powell, CPA
Lay Preacher
Host of The Collect Call *podcast*
Lexington, Kentucky

Questions

How has God answered your prayers in unexpected ways?

Have you ever run away from an answered prayer?

Prayer

God, help me to keep my eyes open for the large and the small blessings you place in my path every day, and once I find them, help me open my heart so that I can allow them inside. *Amen.*

Acts 12:20-25

²⁰Now Herod was angry with the people of Tyre and Sidon. So they came to him in a body; and after winning over Blastus, the king's chamberlain, they asked for a reconciliation, because their country depended on the king's country for food. ²¹On an appointed day Herod put on his royal robes, took his seat on the platform, and delivered a public address to them. ²²The people kept shouting, "The voice of a god, and not of a mortal!"

²³And immediately, because he had not given the glory to God, an angel of the Lord struck him down, and he was eaten by worms and died.

²⁴But the word of God continued to advance and gain adherents. ²⁵Then after completing their mission Barnabas and Saul returned to Jerusalem and brought with them John, whose other name was Mark.

Reflection

With fine irony, Luke tells us the story of the inglorious death of Herod Agrippa, a ruler so fearsome that, in order to get what they needed, the people of Tyre and Sidon shouted out that he was a god. Luke doesn't say how Herod felt about this attributed glory, but apparently he was happy to accept their adulation. Such arrogance proves his downfall, as he is struck by a sudden illness (involving worms!) and dies. Thus the glory of a human "god" is ignominiously demonstrated to be a false idol.

Meanwhile, God's word, which rulers and powerful ones have tried to suppress through orders, arrests, and executions, will not be silent. Hidden like the sower's seed of Luke 8:4-15, which fell in good soil, grew, and produced a hundredfold, God's word has been blossoming in the hearts of those who "bear fruit with patient endurance." The word of God does not flourish in gaudy spectacles of blazing power; such false claims to glory will eventually be revealed for what they are: fraud and corruption. No, the word of God grows in the hearts of those who "hold it fast in an honest and good heart"—and those bearers of God's word will go into all the world and transform it with God's love.

The kingdom of God, we discover, is revealed not in glory, not in self-serving claims of power, not in the adulation of crowds who want something for themselves, but rather in simple ways: love, care, devotion to God's mission in the world. The word of God will not be silent, and the powers of this world cannot overcome it.

The Rev. Canon Susan Brown Snook
Canon for Church Growth and Development, Diocese of Oklahoma
Oklahoma City, Oklahoma

A Journey Through Acts

Questions _____

Where in our world do you see arrogant claims to glory that seem antithetical to the word of God?

Where do you see God's word flourishing in quiet ways? How can you nurture the good seed of the word of God in your own heart?

Prayer _____

Loving God, you have planted your word in our hearts, commanding us to nurture it to bear fruit in our lives and the world. Help us nourish your word so that the world is transformed from glorifying human power to caring for every human, in Jesus' name. *Amen.*

Acts 13:1-12

13 Now in the church at Antioch there were prophets and teachers: Barnabas, Simeon who was called Niger, Lucius of Cyrene, Manaen a member of the court of Herod the ruler, and Saul. ²While they were worshiping the Lord and fasting, the Holy Spirit said, "Set apart for me Barnabas and Saul for the work to which I have called them." ³Then after fasting and praying they laid their hands on them and sent them off.

⁴So, being sent out by the Holy Spirit, they went down to Seleucia; and from there they sailed to Cyprus. ⁵When they arrived at Salamis, they proclaimed the word of God in the synagogues of the Jews. And they had John also to assist them. ⁶When they had gone through the whole island as far as Paphos, they met a certain magician, a Jewish false prophet, named Bar-Jesus. ⁷He was with the proconsul, Sergius Paulus, an intelligent man, who summoned Barnabas and Saul and wanted to hear the word of God. ⁸But the magician Elymas (for that is the translation of his name) opposed them and tried to turn the proconsul away from the faith. ⁹But Saul, also known as Paul, filled with the Holy Spirit, looked intently at him ¹⁰and said, "You son of the devil, you enemy of all righteousness, full of all deceit and villainy, will you not stop making crooked the straight paths of the Lord? ¹¹And now listen—the hand of the Lord is against you, and you will be blind for a while, unable to see the sun." Immediately mist and darkness came over him, and he went about groping for someone to lead him by the hand. ¹²When the proconsul saw what had happened, he believed, for he was astonished at the teaching about the Lord.

Reflection

The second half of Acts opens with a transition. No longer will the story concentrate on the work of the apostles near Jerusalem. Now the gospel will spread, as Jesus commanded: "You will receive power when the Holy Spirit has come upon you; and you will be my witnesses in Jerusalem, in all Judea and Samaria, and to the ends of the earth" (Acts 1:8). The Holy Spirit comes upon the leaders in Antioch during worship and sends Barnabas and Saul forth to proclaim Jesus to the Gentiles.

With this new step, we see a transformation in Saul. From this point forward, he will be known by his Roman name, Paul, as he becomes the apostle to the Gentiles. Given authority by the Holy Spirit, he can read the hearts of others, as he looks intently at Elymas the magician and names the evil he sees. Elymas is struck blind as Saul had been, perhaps in the hope that he too will discover faith in Jesus. Luke doesn't tell us more about Elymas, but we marvel with the proconsul at the power of God and see faith dawn in this powerful Roman official—one of many to hear the good news from Paul.

The mission grows; the good news of Jesus spreads. Spiritual power is not limited to those who knew Jesus in person; authority is passed on to others, down to our own day, through the power of the Holy Spirit. The gospel does not ask us to rest quietly in comfortable places; it calls us, like Paul and Barnabas, to take dangerous and unknown steps into new arenas of proclamation and ministry.

The Rev. Canon Susan Brown Snook
Canon for Church Growth and Development, Diocese of Oklahoma
Oklahoma City, Oklahoma

Questions

Where have you seen the power and authority of the Holy Spirit passed on to others? Where have you experienced that power in your own life?

What arena of ministry might the Holy Spirit be calling you to enter now?

Prayer

Gracious Holy Spirit, you gave your authority to the apostles so that many might know the love of Christ, including me. Grant me the power to discern your will in my life, that I might proclaim God's love as you have called me to do, in Jesus' name. *Amen.*

Acts 13:13-52

¹³Then Paul and his companions set sail from Paphos and came to Perga in Pamphylia. John, however, left them and returned to Jerusalem; ¹⁴but they went on from Perga and came to Antioch in Pisidia. And on the sabbath day they went into the synagogue and sat down. ¹⁵After the reading of the law and the prophets, the officials of the synagogue sent them a message, saying, "Brothers, if you have any word of exhortation for the people, give it." ¹⁶So Paul stood up and with a gesture began to speak:

"You Israelites, and others who fear God, listen. ¹⁷The God of this people Israel chose our ancestors and made the people great during their stay in the land of Egypt, and with uplifted arm he led them out of it. ¹⁸For about forty years he put up with them in the wilderness. ¹⁹After he had destroyed seven nations in the land of Canaan, he gave them their land as an inheritance ²⁰for about four hundred fifty years. After that he gave them judges until the time of the prophet Samuel. ²¹Then they asked for a king; and God gave them Saul son of Kish, a man of the tribe of Benjamin, who reigned for forty years. ²²When he had removed him, he made David their king. In his testimony about him he said, 'I have found David, son of Jesse, to be a man after my heart, who will carry out all my wishes.' ²³Of this man's posterity God has brought to Israel a Savior, Jesus, as he promised; ²⁴before his coming John had already proclaimed a baptism of repentance to all the people of Israel. ²⁵And as John was finishing his work, he said, 'What do you suppose that I am? I am not he. No, but one is coming after me; I am not worthy to untie the thong of the sandals on his feet."

26 "My brothers, you descendants of Abraham's family, and others who fear God, to us the message of this salvation has been sent. 27 Because the residents of Jerusalem and their leaders did not recognize him or understand the words of the prophets that are read every sabbath, they fulfilled those words by condemning him. 28 Even though they found no cause for a sentence of death, they asked Pilate to have him killed. 29 When they had carried out everything that was written about him, they took him down from the tree and laid him in a tomb. 30 But God raised him from the dead; 31 and for many days he appeared to those who came up with him from Galilee to Jerusalem, and they are now his witnesses to the people. 32 And we bring you the good news that what God promised to our ancestors 33 he has fulfilled for us, their children, by raising Jesus; as also it is written in the second psalm,

'You are my Son;
    today I have begotten
        you.'

34 As to his raising him from the dead, no more to return to corruption, he has spoken in this way,

'I will give you the holy
    promises made to
        David.'

35 Therefore he has also said in another psalm,

'You will not let your Holy
    One experience
        corruption.'

36 For David, after he had served the purpose of God in his own generation, died, was laid beside his ancestors, and experienced corruption; 37 but he whom God raised up experienced no corruption. 38 Let it be known to you therefore, my brothers, that through this man forgiveness of sins is proclaimed to you; 39 by this Jesus everyone who believes is set free from all those sins from which you could not be freed

by the law of Moses. ⁴⁰Beware, therefore, that what the prophets said does not happen to you:

⁴¹'Look, you scoffers!
    Be amazed and perish,
for in your days I am doing
        a work,
    a work that you will
        never believe, even if
        someone tells you.'"

⁴²As Paul and Barnabas were going out, the people urged them to speak about these things again the next sabbath. ⁴³When the meeting of the synagogue broke up, many Jews and devout converts to Judaism followed Paul and Barnabas, who spoke to them and urged them to continue in the grace of God.

⁴⁴The next sabbath almost the whole city gathered to hear the word of the Lord. ⁴⁵But when the Jews saw the crowds, they were filled with jealousy; and blaspheming, they contradicted what was spoken by Paul. ⁴⁶Then both Paul and Barnabas spoke out boldly, saying, "It was necessary that the word of God should be spoken first to you. Since you reject it and judge yourselves to be unworthy of eternal life, we are now turning to the Gentiles. ⁴⁷For so the Lord has commanded us, saying,

'I have set you to be a light
    for the Gentiles, so that you
    may bring salvation to the
    ends of the earth.'"

⁴⁸When the Gentiles heard this, they were glad and praised the word of the Lord; and as many as had been destined for eternal life became believers. ⁴⁹Thus the word of the Lord spread throughout the region. ⁵⁰But the Jews incited the devout women of high standing and the leading men of the city, and stirred up persecution against Paul and Barnabas, and drove them out of their region. ⁵¹So they shook the dust off their feet in protest against them, and went to Iconium. ⁵²And the disciples were filled with joy and with the Holy Spirit.

Reflection

Today's passage introduces the many experiences of persecution the apostle Paul faced during his ministry. The story is especially relevant in an age when strongly opinionated people persecute others because their zealous faith leaves no room for God to act in a way that is outside their particular expectations or tradition. Remember: Paul was persecuted by zealots who objected to his inclusive gospel message, not Roman officials trying to repress Christianity.

The text indicates that the religious authorities were jealous that many Gentiles showed up to hear Paul's sermon on the following sabbath. They then became angrier when Paul insisted that although the covenant was given to the Jews, Gentiles are included in the fulfillment of the covenant. The translation that renders the Greek to *jealous* is perfectly correct in the context, but it is helpful to know that the root word here can also be translated as zealous.

I see similar jealousy/zeal manifest in ISIS or Al-Qaeda followers who are intolerant of anyone who does not subscribe to their particular understanding of Islam, even other Muslims! I have also experienced the same kind of zealous exclusivity among Christians unwilling to consider that God might possibly be at work in people who think and pray differently than they do.

Inclusion of non-Jews in God's plan of salvation was just too difficult for many Jews to accept in apostolic times. Still today, God's people struggle with issues of inclusivity: Pentecostals accepting Catholics, Syrian Orthodox accepting Pentecostals, Anglicans accepting each other. How open are we to allowing God to work in peoples' lives differently than God is working in ours?

The Ven. Canon Bill Schwartz, OBE
Archdeacon of the Arabian Gulf Countries
Diocese of Cyprus and the Gulf
Qatar

Questions

When was the last time you experienced the presence of God in a worship tradition unfamiliar to you?

How many Muslims, Hindus, Sikhs, or even Zoroastrians do you count as good friends?

Prayer

Dear Father in Heaven, you love all you created. Increase in me the love of Christ, that I may love the stranger just as Christ loved me, a sinner saved by your grace. *Amen.*

Acts 14:1-20

14 The same thing occurred in Iconium, where Paul and Barnabas went into the Jewish synagogue and spoke in such a way that a great number of both Jews and Greeks became believers. ²But the unbelieving Jews stirred up the Gentiles and poisoned their minds against the brothers. ³So they remained for a long time, speaking boldly for the Lord, who testified to the word of his grace by granting signs and wonders to be done through them. ⁴But the residents of the city were divided; some sided with the Jews, and some with the apostles. ⁵And when an attempt was made by both Gentiles and Jews, with their rulers, to mistreat them and to stone them, ⁶the apostles learned of it and fled to Lystra and Derbe, cities of Lycaonia, and to the surrounding country; ⁷and there they continued proclaiming the good news.

⁸In Lystra there was a man sitting who could not use his feet and had never walked, for he had been crippled from birth. ⁹He listened to Paul as he was speaking. And Paul, looking at him intently and seeing that he had faith to be healed, ¹⁰said in a loud voice, "Stand upright on your feet." And the man sprang up and began to walk. ¹¹When the crowds saw what Paul had done, they shouted in the Lycaonian language, "The gods have come down to us in human form!" ¹²Barnabas they called Zeus, and Paul they called Hermes, because he was the chief speaker. ¹³The priest of Zeus, whose temple was just outside the city, brought oxen and garlands to the gates; he and the crowds wanted to offer sacrifice. ¹⁴When the apostles Barnabas and Paul heard of it, they tore their clothes and rushed out into the crowd, shouting, ¹⁵"Friends,

why are you doing this? We are mortals just like you, and we bring you good news, that you should turn from these worthless things to the living God, who made the heaven and the earth and the sea and all that is in them. ¹⁶In past generations he allowed all the nations to follow their own ways; ¹⁷yet he has not left himself without a witness in doing good—giving you rains from heaven and fruitful seasons, and filling you with food and your hearts with joy."

¹⁸Even with these words, they scarcely restrained the crowds from offering sacrifice to them.

¹⁹But Jews came there from Antioch and Iconium and won over the crowds. Then they stoned Paul and dragged him out of the city, supposing that he was dead. ²⁰But when the disciples surrounded him, he got up and went into the city. The next day he went on with Barnabas to Derbe.

Reflection

"The same thing occurred in...." I can't help but wonder how many times Paul thought, "Here we go again!" as he was persecuted again and again throughout the rest of his life by zealots who objected to his preaching that God's covenant could be extended to all people. Like today's zealots, they not only persecuted Paul personally, but his enemies also did everything they could to discredit him and persuade others that their persecution of Paul was right and good. In some ways, nothing has changed over the past two millennia. We see this expression of zeal most notably today in those who identify with ISIS, Boko Haram, Al-Qaeda, the KKK and other extremists.

It's a mistake to conclude that zeal is undesirable. After all, Paul's zealous commitment to preach the gospel in the face of so much persecution is the singular personal characteristic by which he is known and admired. It is also misleading to easily recognize overzealousness in others because of the intensity or scale of misdirected zeal, while at the same time not allowing ourselves to be challenged to consider how zealous we should be, and how our zeal either expresses or betrays the gospel message.

The testimony of signs and wonders is not the message of salvation. Often signs and wonders are misappropriated or misunderstood, as we read in today's text. God's unconditional, unlimited love and forgiveness is the essence of Good News for all people. If only all people who believe they are acting in God's name would act in God's love.

The Ven. Canon Bill Schwartz, OBE
Archdeacon of the Arabian Gulf Countries
Diocese of Cyprus and the Gulf
Qatar

Questions

Am I zealous about communicating the gospel in all that I say and do? Does my zeal sometimes turn to expressing a message of what I am *against* rather than what I am *for*?

How do we recognize when God is doing something new?

Prayer

Heavenly Father, show me when my communication with others negates my intention to exemplify the love of Christ in my relationships. May my love for you overflow to loving those you love, especially those who do not yet recognize or experience your love in their lives. *Amen.*

Acts 14:21-28

²¹After they had proclaimed the good news to that city and had made many disciples, they returned to Lystra, then on to Iconium and Antioch. ²²There they strengthened the souls of the disciples and encouraged them to continue in the faith, saying, "It is through many persecutions that we must enter the kingdom of God." ²³And after they had appointed elders for them in each church, with prayer and fasting they entrusted them to the Lord in whom they had come to believe.

²⁴Then they passed through Pisidia and came to Pamphylia. ²⁵When they had spoken the word in Perga, they went down to Attalia. ²⁶From there they sailed back to Antioch, where they had been commended to the grace of God for the work that they had completed. ²⁷When they arrived, they called the church together and related all that God had done with them, and how he had opened a door of faith for the Gentiles. ²⁸And they stayed there with the disciples for some time.

Reflection

"They called the church together and related all that God had done with them." These words remind me what church should look like: a coming together of the body, to share and hear what God is doing, how God opened doors of faith. We are all called by name to evangelize and make disciples. We are called, like Paul and Barnabas, to strengthen the souls and encourage others to continue in the faith. Imagine our church filled with disciples praying and entrusting leaders to God and supporting them as they do their work. That is not something we only have to imagine.

I have seen and read "Be the change!" all over and have wondered what that would look like. What would my own home look like if instead of *regañando* (scolding) I would sit with my son to encourage and strengthen him with words that help him continue in the faith? What would it be like if instead of starting vestry or staff meetings with needs and concerns we could start with affirmations and testimonies that fortify and sustain? I wonder if others would start doing the same.

"With prayer and fasting they entrusted them." I don't do very well with fasting but I pray all day long. When I was about sixteen I learned to have ongoing conversation with God. It is amazing that we have a God who hears us, even at a stop sign, even while getting a tattoo (It was three hours long and painful!), even when we don't know what to say. Let's be people who pray, encourage, and tell others what God has done.

Sandra T. Montes, EdD
Spanish Language Consultant
Episcopal Church Foundation
Sugar Land, Texas

Questions_____

How can you be an empowering encourager and relater of good news?

In what areas of your life can you see God opening doors?

Prayer _____

Amado Dios who opens doors of faith, help us encourage and strengthen others for your service. Help us to share with others what you have done in our lives to give hope. Help us be the change you and we long for. *En tu nombre, Amén.*

Acts 15:1-21

15 Then certain individuals came down from Judea and were teaching the brothers, "Unless you are circumcised according to the custom of Moses, you cannot be saved." ²And after Paul and Barnabas had no small dissension and debate with them, Paul and Barnabas and some of the others were appointed to go up to Jerusalem to discuss this question with the apostles and the elders. ³So they were sent on their way by the church, and as they passed through both Phoenicia and Samaria, they reported the conversion of the Gentiles, and brought great joy to all the believers. ⁴When they came to Jerusalem, they were welcomed by the church and the apostles and the elders, and they reported all that God had done with them. ⁵But some believers who belonged to the sect of the Pharisees stood up and said,

"It is necessary for them to be circumcised and ordered to keep the law of Moses."

⁶The apostles and the elders met together to consider this matter. ⁷After there had been much debate, Peter stood up and said to them, "My brothers, you know that in the early days God made a choice among you, that I should be the one through whom the Gentiles would hear the message of the good news and become believers. ⁸And God, who knows the human heart, testified to them by giving them the Holy Spirit, just as he did to us; ⁹and in cleansing their hearts by faith he has made no distinction between them and us. ¹⁰Now therefore why are you putting God to the test by placing on the neck of the disciples a yoke that neither our ancestors nor we have been able to bear? ¹¹On the contrary, we believe that we will

be saved through the grace of the Lord Jesus, just as they will."

[12]The whole assembly kept silence, and listened to Barnabas and Paul as they told of all the signs and wonders that God had done through them among the Gentiles. [13]After they finished speaking, James replied, "My brothers, listen to me. [14]Simeon has related how God first looked favorably on the Gentiles, to take from among them a people for his name. [15]This agrees with the words of the prophets, as it is written,

[16]'After this I will return,
   and I will rebuild the
      dwelling of David,
         which has fallen;
      from its ruins I will
         rebuild it,
      and I will set it up,

[17]so that all other peoples
      may seek the Lord—
   even all the Gentiles over
      whom my name has
      been called.
   Thus says the Lord,
      who has been making
      these things [18]known
      from long ago.'

[19]Therefore I have reached the decision that we should not trouble those Gentiles who are turning to God, [20]but we should write to them to abstain only from things polluted by idols and from fornication and from whatever has been strangled and from blood. [21]For in every city, for generations past, Moses has had those who proclaim him, for he has been read aloud every sabbath in the synagogues."

Reflection

I grew up Evangelical. I grew up hearing from an all-male leadership that I was not supposed to dance, dress a certain way, drink alcohol, smoke, or curse, among many other things. One pastor called most things "satanic," including music and some books. I remember sometimes pushing back on those rules that I did not understand and being chastised for questioning them. I am glad my parents raised me differently. Although there were faith-based rules (my dad is a priest, after all), they also explained those that did not make sense to me. I remember my mom saying that God speaks to everyone differently and loves us all the same. We came to the Episcopal Church in 1986, and since then I have seen God's grace in my life and in others'. We were welcomed and embraced.

When I started working for the Episcopal Church Foundation, I interviewed many people and always asked, including newly elected Presiding Bishop Curry, "What does it mean to be Episcopalian?" The answers were all about acceptance, inclusion, and love. Bishop Curry said, "To be a person who is defined by love for God and love for our neighbor, who is everybody!" This passage from Acts reminds me of that. Nobody I interviewed said that the cornerstones of the Episcopal faith are scripture, tradition, and reason. Nobody talked about the canons or the governance. Nobody said, "Unless you do this or that, you can't be part of the church." I am grateful God knows our heart and saves us by grace, not by anything we may or may not do. As Christians, we are called to welcome all. Some call that radical welcome.

Sandra T. Montes, EdD
Spanish Language Consultant
Episcopal Church Foundation
Sugar Land, Texas

Questions

Have you experienced welcome in the church?

Are there rules we can let go of so we can practice radical welcome?

Prayer

Amado Dios, who knows our human hearts and shows us grace, help us love you, ourselves, and our neighbors. Help us to be radical welcomers to all who may be seeking love, acceptance, and hope. *En tu nombre, Amén.*

Acts 15:22-35

²²Then the apostles and the elders, with the consent of the whole church, decided to choose men from among their members and to send them to Antioch with Paul and Barnabas. They sent Judas called Barsabbas, and Silas, leaders among the brothers, ²³with the following letter: "The brothers, both the apostles and the elders, to the believers of Gentile origin in Antioch and Syria and Cilicia, greetings. ²⁴Since we have heard that certain persons who have gone out from us, though with no instructions from us, have said things to disturb you and have unsettled your minds, ²⁵we have decided unanimously to choose representatives and send them to you, along with our beloved Barnabas and Paul, ²⁶who have risked their lives for the sake of our Lord Jesus Christ. ²⁷We have therefore sent Judas and Silas, who themselves will tell you the same things by word of mouth. ²⁸For it has seemed good to the Holy Spirit and to us to impose on you no further burden than these essentials: ²⁹that you abstain from what has been sacrificed to idols and from blood and from what is strangled and from fornication. If you keep yourselves from these, you will do well. Farewell."

³⁰So they were sent off and went down to Antioch. When they gathered the congregation together, they delivered the letter. ³¹When its members read it, they rejoiced at the exhortation. ³²Judas and Silas, who were themselves prophets, said much to encourage and strengthen the believers. ³³After they had been there for some time, they were sent off in peace by the believers to those who had sent them. ³⁵But Paul and Barnabas remained in Antioch, and there, with many others, they taught and proclaimed the word of the Lord.

Reflection

We continue to read about the ways that the early church embraced change. Led by the Holy Spirit, that community realized that Gentiles were to be included in their fellowship. It may be hard for us to imagine now, but this was a really big deal for those first Christians, as it dawned on them that the love of God was broader and more inclusive than they had ever imagined or had ever been taught.

That process of change came, as it often does, in stages, as you've noticed in previous readings. It started with a vision that came to Peter. He then explained that vision to church leaders. Perhaps they wondered whether Peter had gone off the deep end. They became convinced that Peter's vision was a reflection of the Spirit's leading. So they recruited folks to accompany Paul and Barnabas to proclaim and explain this new understanding, to help people work through the change.

Change is never easy. (As Dilbert says: "Change is good. You go first.") That's especially true in religious communities, and in a denomination that values tradition. But we worship a God who is making all things new. We follow a teacher who was always expanding the vision of who is included in the movement he led. And so by the Spirit, we are always listening and preparing for the new thing God has in mind, and for the amazing fact that God chooses to use us in the process.

The Rev. Jay Sidebotham
Director of RenewalWorks, a ministry of Forward Movement
Wilmington, North Carolina

Questions_____

As you look back on your life, how have your heart and mind been changed? What were the influences that caused you to change, the people or events?

Are you aware of areas that might be growth opportunities for you right now?

Do you sense inner resistance? Can you ask the Spirit to guide you in that process?

Prayer _____

Gracious God, give us grace to be open to the new thing you have for us. Help us listen for how you speak through others, those graced with wider, wiser perspective. Then use us as instruments of your saving activity in the world, sharing a broader vision of love, in the name of Jesus who stretched out arms of love on the cross, to draw us into saving embrace. *Amen.*

Acts 15:36-41

³⁶After some days Paul said to Barnabas, "Come, let us return and visit the believers in every city where we proclaimed the word of the Lord and see how they are doing." ³⁷Barnabas wanted to take with them John called Mark. ³⁸But Paul decided not to take with them one who had deserted them in Pamphylia and had not accompanied them in the work. ³⁹The disagreement became so sharp that they parted company; Barnabas took Mark with him and sailed away to Cyprus. ⁴⁰But Paul chose Silas and set out, the believers commending him to the grace of the Lord. ⁴¹He went through Syria and Cilicia, strengthening the churches.

Reflection

We don't know how much of Jesus' teaching Paul actually heard. But I wouldn't be surprised if he knew the teaching offered when Jesus sent out his disciples, insisting they go out two by two.

As Paul's itinerant, entrepreneurial ministry unfolded, moving from city to city, he always went accompanied by others. He started out traveling with Barnabas, a supporting actor in the New Testament drama. Barnabas' significance is signaled by the fact that his name was changed by his community. The new name given him meant "son of encouragement." What a great name to be given by your community!

Barnabas probably needed to draw on that new name often. Paul might not have been the easiest traveling companion. In today's reading, a sharp disagreement arises between Paul and Barnabas. Ultimately, they parted ways.

But they each continued in ministry, with new partners. In the mystery of God's work in the world, I wonder if their disagreement actually broadened the impact of their ministries and helped the church grow.

God places us in community, calling us to work side by side with people we might not have chosen. Maybe they're folks we don't even like. Disagreements will arise in the church. (How's that for a news flash?) Yet we can take comfort that God will accomplish God's purposes. Our disagreements can be redeemed and even contribute to the furtherance of the gospel. In it and through it all, we claim the good news that God is at work.

The Rev. Jay Sidebotham
Director of RenewalWorks, a ministry of Forward Movement
Wilmington, North Carolina

A Journey Through Acts

Questions _____

If your community was going to give you a new name that described your character, what might that name be?

How have you handled disagreements in the community? What have been the lessons learned? How have you arrived at resolution?

When in the community have you had the opportunity to extend forgiveness? When have you received it?

Prayer _____

Gracious God, you call us into community, often a source of joy and comfort, often a growth opportunity. Help us to recognize our part when disagreement and conflict arise. Teach us to make amends. Bless us with reconciling love and a spirit of encouragement. Then send us out into the world this day to do the loving work you have given us to do. *Amen.*

Acts 16:1-15

16 Paul went on also to Derbe and to Lystra, where there was a disciple named Timothy, the son of a Jewish woman who was a believer; but his father was a Greek. ²He was well spoken of by the believers in Lystra and Iconium. ³Paul wanted Timothy to accompany him; and he took him and had him circumcised because of the Jews who were in those places, for they all knew that his father was a Greek. ⁴As they went from town to town, they delivered to them for observance the decisions that had been reached by the apostles and elders who were in Jerusalem. ⁵So the churches were strengthened in the faith and increased in numbers daily.

⁶They went through the region of Phrygia and Galatia, having been forbidden by the Holy Spirit to speak the word in Asia. ⁷When they had come opposite Mysia, they attempted to go into Bithynia, but the Spirit of Jesus did not allow them; ⁸so, passing by Mysia, they went down to Troas. ⁹During the night Paul had a vision: there stood a man of Macedonia pleading with him and saying, "Come over to Macedonia and help us." ¹⁰When he had seen the vision, we immediately tried to cross over to Macedonia, being convinced that God had called us to proclaim the good news to them.

¹¹We set sail from Troas and took a straight course to Samothrace, the following day to Neapolis, ¹²and from there to Philippi, which is a leading city of the district of Macedonia and a Roman colony. We remained in this city for some days. ¹³On the sabbath day we went outside the gate by the river, where we supposed there was a place of prayer; and we sat down and spoke

to the women who had gathered there. [14]A certain woman named Lydia, a worshiper of God, was listening to us; she was from the city of Thyatira and a dealer in purple cloth. The Lord opened her heart to listen eagerly to what was said by Paul. [15]When she and her household were baptized, she urged us, saying, "If you have judged me to be faithful to the Lord, come and stay at my home." And she prevailed upon us.

Reflection

Paul's missionary journeys are accounted for here in amazing fashion. Luke is sharing this information with us for theological purposes and not for us to put together a chronological timeline or for historical context. Paul, in a few verses, here is shown to travel thousands of miles and maybe out of order compared to the accounts Paul gives us in his letters. But the point is for us to realize how God works in our lives. When we encounter barriers, when we encounter hardship, persecution, or even the inability to speak the gospel, showing up is important!

When Paul showed up, the Holy Spirit strengthened the people of the churches. Sometimes it was not about what he said or preached or taught. It was about showing up and being present to the Holy Spirit and those who were in need.

Hearts are softened through the power of the Holy Spirit, and through our willingness to be present and show up among others. People are encouraged through relationship. Lydia personifies the courage to engage the power of the Holy Spirit and to reach out to others in gracious hospitality. Hospitality takes a listening heart and ear as well as an invitation to come and stay with each other in heart, mind, soul, and strength.

Paul's journey and Lydia's hospitality share with us the power of God's presence in our lives and the need for us to share that love and grace with others. There is a sense of immediacy needed for us to share and to work for the kingdom; there is a sense that others need God's love and grace. May we make it so!

The Very Rev. Justin Alan Lindstrom
Dean, Saint Paul's Cathedral
Oklahoma City, Oklahoma

A Journey Through Acts

Questions _____

What are the barriers you face? How can the Holy Spirit help you overcome them?

How do you share the gospel with others?

Prayer _____

O God of grace, give us courage to make our journey and to trust in your bountiful Spirit, that even in the face of hardship and difficulty, the Holy Spirit overcomes our weaknesses and gives us the strength to be your people. Guide us in the way of compassion and hospitality that all may come to know your saving embrace. *Amen.*

Acts 16:16-40

¹⁶One day, as we were going to the place of prayer, we met a slave girl who had a spirit of divination and brought her owners a great deal of money by fortune-telling. ¹⁷While she followed Paul and us, she would cry out, "These men are slaves of the Most High God, who proclaim to you a way of salvation." ¹⁸She kept doing this for many days. But Paul, very much annoyed, turned and said to the spirit, "I order you in the name of Jesus Christ to come out of her." And it came out that very hour.

¹⁹But when her owners saw that their hope of making money was gone, they seized Paul and Silas and dragged them into the marketplace before the authorities. ²⁰When they had brought them before the magistrates, they said, "These men are disturbing our city; they are Jews ²¹and are advocating customs that are not lawful for us as Romans to adopt or observe." ²²The crowd joined in attacking them, and the magistrates had them stripped of their clothing and ordered them to be beaten with rods. ²³After they had given them a severe flogging, they threw them into prison and ordered the jailer to keep them securely. ²⁴Following these instructions, he put them in the innermost cell and fastened their feet in the stocks.

²⁵About midnight Paul and Silas were praying and singing hymns to God, and the prisoners were listening to them. ²⁶Suddenly there was an earthquake, so violent that the foundations of the prison were shaken; and immediately all the doors were opened and everyone's chains were unfastened. ²⁷When the jailer woke up and saw the prison doors wide open, he drew his

sword and was about to kill himself, since he supposed that the prisoners had escaped. [28]But Paul shouted in a loud voice, "Do not harm yourself, for we are all here." [29]The jailer called for lights, and rushing in, he fell down trembling before Paul and Silas. [30]Then he brought them outside and said, "Sirs, what must I do to be saved?" [31]They answered, "Believe on the Lord Jesus, and you will be saved, you and your household." [32]They spoke the word of the Lord to him and to all who were in his house. [33]At the same hour of the night he took them and washed their wounds; then he and his entire family were baptized without delay. [34]He brought them up into the house and set food before them; and he and his entire household rejoiced that he had become a believer in God.

[35]When morning came, the magistrates sent the police, saying, "Let those men go." [36]And the jailer reported the message to Paul, saying, "The magistrates sent word to let you go; therefore come out now and go in peace." [37]But Paul replied, "They have beaten us in public, uncondemned, men who are Roman citizens, and have thrown us into prison; and now are they going to discharge us in secret? Certainly not! Let them come and take us out themselves." [38]The police reported these words to the magistrates, and they were afraid when they heard that they were Roman citizens; [39]so they came and apologized to them. And they took them out and asked them to leave the city. [40]After leaving the prison they went to Lydia's home; and when they had seen and encouraged the brothers and sisters there, they departed.

Reflection

The livelihood or money-making opportunity of the slave owners was removed through the healing and renewal of a slave girl, and that infuriated them. Money can sometimes get in the way of our healing. The police were called in and Paul and Silas were arrested, found guilty, and imprisoned for doing God's work of liberation, reconciliation, healing, and forgiveness.

The story does not end there. Paul and Silas are down and out, but joyfully singing and praising God in the depths of their prison cell. In the midst of what could be seen as an awful situation, they share the gospel with the other prisoners. There is an earthquake. The cell doors are opened. The chains are rattled free. Yet, everyone stays. It gets better! The jailer comes, thinking he will find an empty prison, and to his surprise he finds everyone present and accounted for. The jailer receives the gospel. Paul and Silas are freed. What an amazing story!

Once again, Luke shows us the power of the gospel and the Holy Spirit at work in our lives. We are imprisoned and there are barriers in our lives that prevent us from fully seeing God's love and grace. When we persevere in prayer, praise, song, and worship, we can come to know the Almighty God in new and amazing ways. The depth and breadth of our faith is transformed, renewed, restored, and strengthened by God's grace. It is then that we might have the courage to share God's love with others and to live into that love more fully in our own lives.

The Very Rev. Justin Alan Lindstrom
Dean, Saint Paul's Cathedral
Oklahoma City, Oklahoma

A Journey Through Acts

Questions _____

When you are faced with tough situations how do you use your spiritual disciplines to access God's grace, love, and presence?

When have you experienced renewal and restoration in your life?

How was God present in those moments? How did you share that with others?

Prayer _____

Holy and gracious God, in your tender mercy guide us and lead us into your blessed presence. Fill us with the courage to be your people, even in moments of despair. Allow us to always sing your praises and know the healing power of the gospel. And, give us the ability to share your love with others. *Amen.*

Acts 17:1-9

17 After Paul and Silas had passed through Amphipolis and Apollonia, they came to Thessalonica, where there was a synagogue of the Jews. 2And Paul went in, as was his custom, and on three sabbath days argued with them from the scriptures, 3explaining and proving that it was necessary for the Messiah to suffer and to rise from the dead, and saying, "This is the Messiah, Jesus whom I am proclaiming to you." 4Some of them were persuaded and joined Paul and Silas, as did a great many of the devout Greeks and not a few of the leading women. 5But the Jews became jealous, and with the help of some ruffians in the marketplaces they formed a mob and set the city in an uproar. While they were searching for Paul and Silas to bring them out to the assembly, they attacked Jason's house. 6When they could not find them, they dragged Jason and some believers before the city authorities, shouting, "These people who have been turning the world upside down have come here also, 7and Jason has entertained them as guests. They are all acting contrary to the decrees of the emperor, saying that there is another king named Jesus." 8The people and the city officials were disturbed when they heard this, 9and after they had taken bail from Jason and the others, they let them go.

Reflection

"These people who have been turning the world upside down have come here also…"

The first Christian believers were not particularly welcomed. They were seen as disturbers of the peace, and even revolutionaries promoting "that there is another king named Jesus." These "Christ followers" were perceived to actually be less than religious, and thus threats to the good order of the empire. The misunderstanding and persecution continued until the conversion of the emperor Constantine several hundred years later. The Edict of Milan, which followed, brought toleration in 313 CE. Over time the Christian faith predominated, becoming the official religion of the Roman Empire. With the rise of the church came the concept of "Christendom"— the kingdom of Christ—which was both a description and a political ideal, applied to the western world.

Over centuries, however, Christendom lost its force, and now scholars tell us we live in a "post-Christian" era. The Christian faith dominated for well over a millennium, but did it really live into the fullness of the message proclaimed in the Acts of the Apostles? Did we forget that the world was turned upside down by followers of a king who ruled from a cross? Did we forget that the king's reign was to bring reconciliation, love, forgiveness, acceptance, and peace in a radical, life-transforming way? The reign of Christ begins with a heart transformed, and with a community of transformed hearts.

Many things still compete for our loyalty, our attention, and our service. Does that world-turning message still hold true? Considering our life together as Christians, can we learn, as did those first believers in Acts, that a world turned upside down in Christ, is really, finally, right side up?

The Very Rev. Steven A. Peay
Dean-President and Professor of Homiletics and Church History
Nashotah House Theological Seminary
Nashotah, Wisconsin

Questions

How has the Good News turned your world upside down?

Where does it still need to be turned?

Prayer

Oh God, you gave those first Christian believers great faith, insight, and courage through the Holy Spirit, to be witnesses to your Son Jesus, and the truth of his gospel. Help us to be bold in our witness, that the world may be turned upside down, in Jesus' Name. *Amen.*

Acts 17:10-34

[10]That very night the believers sent Paul and Silas off to Beroea; and when they arrived, they went to the Jewish synagogue. [11]These Jews were more receptive than those in Thessalonica, for they welcomed the message very eagerly and examined the scriptures every day to see whether these things were so. [12]Many of them therefore believed, including not a few Greek women and men of high standing. [13]But when the Jews of Thessalonica learned that the word of God had been proclaimed by Paul in Beroea as well, they came there too, to stir up and incite the crowds. [14]Then the believers immediately sent Paul away to the coast, but Silas and Timothy remained behind. [15]Those who conducted Paul brought him as far as Athens; and after receiving instructions to have Silas and Timothy join him as soon as possible, they left him.

[16]While Paul was waiting for them in Athens, he was deeply distressed to see that the city was full of idols. [17]So he argued in the synagogue with the Jews and the devout persons, and also in the marketplace every day with those who happened to be there. [18]Also some Epicurean and Stoic philosophers debated with him. Some said, "What does this babbler want to say?" Others said, "He seems to be a proclaimer of foreign divinities." (This was because he was telling the good news about Jesus and the resurrection.) [19]So they took him and brought him to the Areopagus and asked him, "May we know what this new teaching is that you are presenting? [20]It sounds rather strange to us, so we would like to know what it means." [21]Now all the Athenians

and the foreigners living there would spend their time in nothing but telling or hearing something new.

²²Then Paul stood in front of the Areopagus and said, "Athenians, I see how extremely religious you are in every way. ²³For as I went through the city and looked carefully at the objects of your worship, I found among them an altar with the inscription, 'To an unknown god.' What therefore you worship as unknown, this I proclaim to you. ²⁴The God who made the world and everything in it, he who is Lord of heaven and earth, does not live in shrines made by human hands, ²⁵nor is he served by human hands, as though he needed anything, since he himself gives to all mortals life and breath and all things. ²⁶From one ancestor he made all nations to inhabit the whole earth, and he allotted the times of their existence and the boundaries of the places where they would live, ²⁷so that they would search for God and perhaps grope for him and find

him—though indeed he is not far from each one of us. ²⁸For 'In him we live and move and have our being'; as even some of your own poets have said,

'For we too are his offspring.'

²⁹Since we are God's offspring, we ought not to think that the deity is like gold, or silver, or stone, an image formed by the art and imagination of mortals. ³⁰While God has overlooked the times of human ignorance, now he commands all people everywhere to repent, ³¹because he has fixed a day on which he will have the world judged in righteousness by a man whom he has appointed, and of this he has given assurance to all by raising him from the dead."

³²When they heard of the resurrection of the dead, some scoffed; but others said, "We will hear you again about this." ³³At that point Paul left them. ³⁴But some of them joined him and became believers, including Dionysius the Areopagite and a woman named Damaris, and others with them.

Reflection

"Then Paul stood in front of the Areopagus and said, 'Athenians, I see how extremely religious you are in every way.'"

Paul showed his training as both rabbi and as public speaker in his address to the Athenians. Most of us would steer clear of such a topic, following the old adage that religion and politics make for problematic conversations. Yet we are called upon to share our faith and to take up the work of evangelism—spreading the Good News of the faith that we have in Jesus Christ. If Paul had not opened the conversation, he would not have been able to share the Good News of Jesus, crucified and risen.

Let's look at how Paul approaches the topic. First, he starts with where the Athenians are in their own situation. He acknowledges their religiousness, pointing out that their altars cover many deities. "For as I went through the city and looked carefully at the objects of your worship, I found among them an altar with the inscription, 'To an unknown god.' What therefore you worship as unknown, this I proclaim to you" (Acts 17:23). He then opens the door to reveal God as creator. So they see their own tradition tying with the revelation. Paul utilizes their literature in verse 28 "….As even some of your poets have said, 'For we too are his offspring.'" This leads to the proclamation of Jesus as Savior, identifying with the human condition, raising us from death to life.

Some respond negatively. Others want to hear more. Some embrace the message right away. We have to remember that evangelism is the

Holy Spirit's work, ultimately, and we're simply the messengers. The important thing is to be loving, gracious, and kind as we share the message.

The Very Rev. Steven A. Peay
Dean-President and Professor of Homiletics and Church History
Nashotah House Theological Seminary
Nashotah, Wisconsin

Questions

Reflect on how you came to faith—who shared the gospel with you?

How might you share the Good News of Jesus with others?

Prayer

Father, your Son bid us to carry his Good News to the ends of the earth. Send the fire of the Spirit upon us anew, that we, like Paul, may witness boldly, wisely, and lovingly, to our Lord, in whose Name we pray. *Amen*.

Acts 18:1-28

18 After this Paul left Athens and went to Corinth. 2There he found a Jew named Aquila, a native of Pontus, who had recently come from Italy with his wife Priscilla, because Claudius had ordered all Jews to leave Rome. Paul went to see them, 3and, because he was of the same trade, he stayed with them, and they worked together—by trade they were tentmakers. 4Every sabbath he would argue in the synagogue and would try to convince Jews and Greeks. 5When Silas and Timothy arrived from Macedonia, Paul was occupied with proclaiming the word, testifying to the Jews that the Messiah was Jesus. 6When they opposed and reviled him, in protest he shook the dust from his clothes and said to them, "Your blood be on your own heads! I am innocent. From now on I will go to the Gentiles."

7Then he left the synagogue and went to the house of a man named Titius Justus, a worshiper of God; his house was next door to the synagogue. 8Crispus, the official of the synagogue, became a believer in the Lord, together with all his household; and many of the Corinthians who heard Paul became believers and were baptized. 9One night the Lord said to Paul in a vision, "Do not be afraid, but speak and do not be silent; 10for I am with you, and no one will lay a hand on you to harm you, for there are many in this city who are my people." 11He stayed there a year and six months, teaching the word of God among them.

12But when Gallio was proconsul of Achaia, the Jews made a united attack on Paul and brought him before the tribunal. 13They said, "This man is persuading people to worship God in ways that are contrary to the law." [14]Just as Paul was about to speak, Gallio said to the Jews, "If it were a matter of crime or serious villainy, I would be justified in accepting the complaint of you Jews; [15]but since it is a matter of questions about words and names and your own law, see to it yourselves; I do not wish to be a judge of these matters." [16]And he dismissed them from the tribunal. [17]Then all of them seized Sosthenes, the official of the synagogue, and beat him in front of the tribunal. But Gallio paid no attention to any of these things.

[18]After staying there for a considerable time, Paul said farewell to the believers and sailed for Syria, accompanied by Priscilla and Aquila. At Cenchreae he had his hair cut, for he was under a vow. [19]When they reached Ephesus, he left them there, but first he himself went into the synagogue and had a discussion with the Jews. [20]When they asked him to stay longer, he declined; [21]but on taking leave of them, he said, "I will return to you, if God wills." Then he set sail from Ephesus.

[22]When he had landed at Caesarea, he went up to Jerusalem and greeted the church, and then went down to Antioch. [23]After spending some time there he departed and went from place to place through the region of Galatia and Phrygia, strengthening all the disciples.

[24]Now there came to Ephesus a Jew named Apollos, a native of Alexandria. He was an eloquent man, well-versed in the scriptures. [25]He had been instructed in the Way of the Lord; and he spoke with burning enthusiasm and taught accurately the things concerning Jesus, though he knew only the baptism of John. [26]He began to speak boldly in the synagogue; but when Priscilla and Aquila heard him, they took him aside and explained the Way of God to him more accurately. [27]And when he wished to cross over to Achaia, the believers

encouraged him and wrote to the disciples to welcome him. On his arrival he greatly helped those who through grace had become believers, [28]for he powerfully refuted the Jews in public, showing by the scriptures that the Messiah is Jesus.

Reflection

I'm not much of an evangelist—some things Paul says try my patience. Or maybe I'm an introverted evangelist? I want to attract rather than promote. I want my actions to speak. I want to do a spiritual thing and not be found out. I've little truck for converting Muslims or Jews or Buddhists or people of other faiths, which I know some of my brothers and sisters like very much to do. In my own humble witness, that remains too arrogant for the likes of me.

I'll tell you what I have seen: I've seen an empty room in the cathedral here in Madrid grow with twelve-step recovery groups, from two people to over a hundred in three years' time. I hear the word of God in there more than I do in my church office. It's grown much more rapidly than anything happening in our pews. I relate, of course, to people not listening to a message, either in church or in a twelve-step meeting, people that fall away. And in twelve-step communities, some die when they do not listen to the message.

I've seen that. But I'm going to go on faith that God has everyone's back. I believe God loves me, finally, and feel God encouraging me just as he does with Paul in this passage: "Keep on speaking, do not be silent." I'm saying, "*This* has worked for me, maybe it *might* work for you, but if it doesn't, move along, someone else needs to be in that pew or AA meeting, making the coffee."

I too, like Paul, have traveled from place to place in my ministry, from Honduras to Madrid. Paul is a tentmaker. Tents are flimsy and can disappear in the middle of the night. I'm a tentmaker.

The Rev. Spencer Reece
National Secretary for the Bishop of the Episcopal Church of Spain
Madrid, Spain

A Journey Through Acts

Questions:

What does evangelism mean to you?

Can you disagree with Paul and be a Christian?

Prayer:

O Lord, let me move in this world like a tentmaker. *Amen.*

Acts: 19:1—20:16

19 While Apollos was in Corinth, Paul passed through the interior regions and came to Ephesus, where he found some disciples. ²He said to them, "Did you receive the Holy Spirit when you became believers?" They replied, "No, we have not even heard that there is a Holy Spirit." ³Then he said, "Into what then were you baptized?" They answered, "Into John's baptism." ⁴Paul said, "John baptized with the baptism of repentance, telling the people to believe in the one who was to come after him, that is, in Jesus." ⁵On hearing this, they were baptized in the name of the Lord Jesus. ⁶When Paul had laid his hands on them, the Holy Spirit came upon them, and they spoke in tongues and prophesied—⁷altogether there were about twelve of them.

⁸He entered the synagogue and for three months spoke out boldly, and argued persuasively about the kingdom of God. ⁹When some stubbornly refused to believe and spoke evil of the Way before the congregation, he left them, taking the disciples with him, and argued daily in the lecture hall of Tyrannus. ¹⁰This continued for two years, so that all the residents of Asia, both Jews and Greeks, heard the word of the Lord.

¹¹God did extraordinary miracles through Paul, ¹²so that when the handkerchiefs or aprons that had touched his skin were brought to the sick, their diseases left them, and the evil spirits came out of them. ¹³Then some itinerant Jewish exorcists tried to use the name of the Lord Jesus over those who had evil spirits, saying, "I adjure you by the Jesus whom Paul proclaims." ¹⁴Seven sons of a Jewish high priest named Sceva were doing this. ¹⁵But the

evil spirit said to them in reply, "Jesus I know, and Paul I know; but who are you?" [16]Then the man with the evil spirit leaped on them, mastered them all, and so overpowered them that they fled out of the house naked and wounded. [17]When this became known to all residents of Ephesus, both Jews and Greeks, everyone was awestruck; and the name of the Lord Jesus was praised. [18]Also many of those who became believers confessed and disclosed their practices. [19]A number of those who practiced magic collected their books and burned them publicly; when the value of these books was calculated, it was found to come to fifty thousand silver coins. [20]So the word of the Lord grew mightily and prevailed.

[21]Now after these things had been accomplished, Paul resolved in the Spirit to go through Macedonia and Achaia, and then to go on to Jerusalem. He said, "After I have gone there, I must also see Rome." [22]So he sent two of his helpers, Timothy and Erastus, to Macedonia, while he himself stayed for some time longer in Asia.

[23]About that time no little disturbance broke out concerning the Way. [24]A man named Demetrius, a silversmith who made silver shrines of Artemis, brought no little business to the artisans. [25]These he gathered together, with the workers of the same trade, and said, "Men, you know that we get our wealth from this business. [26]You also see and hear that not only in Ephesus but in almost the whole of Asia this Paul has persuaded and drawn away a considerable number of people by saying that gods made with hands are not gods. [27]And there is danger not only that this trade of ours may come into disrepute but also that the temple of the great goddess Artemis will be scorned, and she will be deprived of her majesty that brought all Asia and the world to worship her."

²⁸When they heard this, they were enraged and shouted, "Great is Artemis of the Ephesians!" ²⁹The city was filled with the confusion; and people rushed together to the theater, dragging with them Gaius and Aristarchus, Macedonians who were Paul's travel companions. ³⁰Paul wished to go into the crowd, but the disciples would not let him; ³¹even some officials of the province of Asia, who were friendly to him, sent him a message urging him not to venture into the theater. ³²Meanwhile, some were shouting one thing, some another; for the assembly was in confusion, and most of them did not know why they had come together. ³³Some of the crowd gave instructions to Alexander, whom the Jews had pushed forward. And Alexander motioned for silence and tried to make a defense before the people. ³⁴But when they recognized that he was a Jew, for about two hours all of them shouted in unison, "Great is Artemis of the Ephesians!" ³⁵But when the town clerk had quieted the crowd, he said, "Citizens of Ephesus, who is there that does not know that the city of the Ephesians is the temple keeper of the great Artemis and of the statue that fell from heaven? ³⁶Since these things cannot be denied, you ought to be quiet and do nothing rash. ³⁷You have brought these men here who are neither temple robbers nor blasphemers of our goddess. ³⁸If therefore Demetrius and the artisans with him have a complaint against anyone, the courts are open, and there are proconsuls; let them bring charges there against one another. ³⁹If there is anything further you want to know, it must be settled in the regular assembly. ⁴⁰For we are in danger of being charged with rioting today, since there is no cause that we can give to justify this commotion." ⁴¹When he had said this, he dismissed the assembly.

20 After the uproar had ceased, Paul sent for the disciples; and after encouraging

them and saying farewell, he left for Macedonia. ²When he had gone through those regions and had given the believers much encouragement, he came to Greece, ³where he stayed for three months. He was about to set sail for Syria when a plot was made against him by the Jews, and so he decided to return through Macedonia. ⁴He was accompanied by Sopater son of Pyrrhus from Beroea, by Aristarchus and Secundus from Thessalonica, by Gaius from Derbe, and by Timothy, as well as by Tychicus and Trophimus from Asia. ⁵They went ahead and were waiting for us in Troas; ⁶but we sailed from Philippi after the days of Unleavened Bread, and in five days we joined them in Troas, where we stayed for seven days.

⁷On the first day of the week, when we met to break bread, Paul was holding a discussion with them; since he intended to leave the next day, he continued speaking until midnight. ⁸There were many lamps in the room upstairs where we were meeting. ⁹A young man named Eutychus, who was sitting in the window, began to sink off into a deep sleep while Paul talked still longer. Overcome by sleep, he fell to the ground three floors below and was picked up dead. ¹⁰But Paul went down, and bending over him took him in his arms, and said, "Do not be alarmed, for his life is in him." ¹¹Then Paul went upstairs, and after he had broken bread and eaten, he continued to converse with them until dawn; then he left. ¹²Meanwhile they had taken the boy away alive and were not a little comforted.

¹³We went ahead to the ship and set sail for Assos, intending to take Paul on board there; for he had made this arrangement, intending to go by land himself. ¹⁴When he met us in Assos, we took him on board and went to Mitylene. ¹⁵We sailed from there, and on the following day we arrived opposite Chios. The next day we touched at Samos,

Reflection

In Acts, love spreads like electricity from town to town. Reading Acts is like standing on a hill and watching an entire city light up, town by town. Once when I flew back from Lambeth Palace in London in the early morning hours after visiting with the Archbishop of Canterbury, I could see out the plane window the lights of all of Madrid, a city of five million people. I could see all the little towns lit up. Made me think of Acts—believers connecting, believers lighting each other up, illuminating whole towns. And moving from the palace to our humble diocese in Spain, I felt some of that light inside of me.

At the end of Luke's Gospel is the story of the road to Emmaus, and it is thought that the person who wrote Luke also wrote Acts, so Emmaus hinges the two books—hinges the narrative between the life of Christ and what comes after. Emmaus captures achingly clear belief with Cleopus and the unnamed disciple, when their eyes are opened and their hearts burn within them and they realize the man before them is Christ. From that moment on there is no stopping this.

It's a very human moment to realize the thing that has been standing in front of you was pure love only after it is gone. We humans sometimes don't appreciate what is in front of us until it has been removed. That's been my story more times than I wish.

In Acts, we follow Paul, a tenacious evangelizer, sometimes comical in his insistence, shaking out his clothes, writing signs in big block capitals for the Galatians. He seems to be jumping up from scripture and saying, "See! Look at me! Pay attention to this!" I love that in this passage, Eutychus is so bored listening to Paul that he falls asleep and then falls out the window. There's a lot of words in the church, people in love with the sound of their own voices. But acts convince me more.

The Rev. Spencer Reece
National Secretary for the Bishop of the Episcopal Church of Spain
Madrid, Spain

Questions:

What act of another have you seen that brought you to faith?

What could you do rather than say?

Prayer:

Let me do one anonymous act of love today. *Amen.*

Acts 20:17-38

[17]From Miletus [Paul] sent a message to Ephesus, asking the elders of the church to meet him. [18]When they came to him, he said to them:

"You yourselves know how I lived among you the entire time from the first day that I set foot in Asia, [19]serving the Lord with all humility and with tears, enduring the trials that came to me through the plots of the Jews. [20]I did not shrink from doing anything helpful, proclaiming the message to you and teaching you publicly and from house to house, [21]as I testified to both Jews and Greeks about repentance toward God and faith toward our Lord Jesus. [22]And now, as a captive to the Spirit, I am on my way to Jerusalem, not knowing what will happen to me there, [23]except that the Holy Spirit testifies to me in every city that imprisonment and persecutions are waiting for me. [24]But I do not count my life of any value to myself, if only I may finish my course and the ministry that I received from the Lord Jesus, to testify to the good news of God's grace.

[25]"And now I know that none of you, among whom I have gone about proclaiming the kingdom, will ever see my face again. [26]Therefore I declare to you this day that I am not responsible for the blood of any of you, [27]for I did not shrink from declaring to you the whole purpose of God. [28]Keep watch over yourselves and over all the flock, of which the Holy Spirit has made you overseers, to shepherd the church of God that he obtained with the blood of his own Son. [29]I know that after I have gone, savage wolves will come in among you, not sparing the flock. [30]Some even from your own group will

come distorting the truth in order to entice the disciples to follow them. ³¹Therefore be alert, remembering that for three years I did not cease night or day to warn everyone with tears. ³²And now I commend you to God and to the message of his grace, a message that is able to build you up and to give you the inheritance among all who are sanctified. ³³I coveted no one's silver or gold or clothing. ³⁴You know for yourselves that I worked with my own hands to support myself and my companions. ³⁵In all this I have given you an example that by such work we must support the weak, remembering the words of the Lord Jesus, for he himself said, 'It is more blessed to give than to receive.'"

³⁶When he had finished speaking, he knelt down with them all and prayed. ³⁷There was much weeping among them all; they embraced Paul and kissed him, ³⁸grieving especially because of what he had said, that they would not see him again. Then they brought him to the ship.

Reflection

Yesterday, we enjoyed a bit of humor while also noting that some things never change. Church is, if we are honest, occasionally boring now, and apparently it was the same in the time of Paul. You see, while Paul spoke late into the night one evening, a young man named Eutychus fell asleep and, in fact, fell out the window. It's almost a slapstick scene, and we can enjoy it thus because Paul ensures that Eutychus is well. I note this because sometimes we think we need to read the Bible as a very serious book when it is really full of humor at every turn. Read this story with an eye toward the possibility of comedy, and you'll see what I mean.

Today, in quite the opposite of comedy, we read Paul's address to the Ephesian presbyters at Melitus. He is on his way to Jerusalem, and this speech has double poignancy. First, there is the inherent danger of travel: Going on a sea voyage was always risky. Second, Paul expects that things won't go well for him in Jerusalem. But despite the danger and the threat of his own mortality, Paul urges the leaders at Ephesus to be prepared for dangers from within the church as he shares his own calling "to testify to the good news of God's grace."

We don't tend to think of the inside of a church as dangerous, but the fact is that Paul is right. When leaders betray the trust they have been given, souls are endangered and the gospel witness is compromised. Pastors and leaders must always be vigilant.

The Rev. Canon Scott Gunn
Executive Director, Forward Movement
Cincinnati, Ohio

Questions

What do you think prompted Paul's exhortation to the elders from Ephesus?

Paul speaks of his mission to testify to God's grace, and he commends to the elders "the message of [God's] grace." How would you testify to God's grace?

What is the message of grace our world needs to hear?

Prayer

Gracious God, guide us always to see past our fears, our short-comings, and our own desires, so that we might be steadily focused on the gift of your love in Jesus Christ; strengthen us to bear tidings of your grace into the world. Through Christ our Lord. *Amen.*

Acts 21:1-26

21 When we had parted from them and set sail, we came by a straight course to Cos, and the next day to Rhodes, and from there to Patara. ²When we found a ship bound for Phoenicia, we went on board and set sail. ³We came in sight of Cyprus; and leaving it on our left, we sailed to Syria and landed at Tyre, because the ship was to unload its cargo there. ⁴We looked up the disciples and stayed there for seven days. Through the Spirit they told Paul not to go on to Jerusalem. ⁵When our days there were ended, we left and proceeded on our journey; and all of them, with wives and children, escorted us outside the city. There we knelt down on the beach and prayed ⁶and said farewell to one another. Then we went on board the ship, and they returned home.

⁷When we had finished the voyage from Tyre, we arrived at Ptolemais; and we greeted the believers and stayed with them for one day. ⁸The next day we left and came to Caesarea; and we went into the house of Philip the evangelist, one of the seven, and stayed with him. ⁹He had four unmarried daughters who had the gift of prophecy. ¹⁰While we were staying there for several days, a prophet named Agabus came down from Judea. ¹¹He came to us and took Paul's belt, bound his own feet and hands with it, and said, "Thus says the Holy Spirit, 'This is the way the Jews in Jerusalem will bind the man who owns this belt and will hand him over to the Gentiles.'" ¹²When we heard this, we and the people there urged him not to go up to Jerusalem. ¹³Then Paul answered, "What are you doing, weeping and breaking my

heart? For I am ready not only to be bound but even to die in Jerusalem for the name of the Lord Jesus." [14]Since he would not be persuaded, we remained silent except to say, "The Lord's will be done."

[15]After these days we got ready and started to go up to Jerusalem. [16]Some of the disciples from Caesarea also came along and brought us to the house of Mnason of Cyprus, an early disciple, with whom we were to stay.

[17]When we arrived in Jerusalem, the brothers welcomed us warmly. [18]The next day Paul went with us to visit James; and all the elders were present. [19]After greeting them, he related one by one the things that God had done among the Gentiles through his ministry. [20]When they heard it, they praised God. Then they said to him, "You see, brother, how many thousands of believers there are among the Jews, and they are all zealous for the law. [21]They have been told

about you that you teach all the Jews living among the Gentiles to forsake Moses, and that you tell them not to circumcise their children or observe the customs. [22]What then is to be done? They will certainly hear that you have come. [23]So do what we tell you. We have four men who are under a vow. [24]Join these men, go through the rite of purification with them, and pay for the shaving of their heads. Thus all will know that there is nothing in what they have been told about you, but that you yourself observe and guard the law. [25]But as for the Gentiles who have become believers, we have sent a letter with our judgment that they should abstain from what has been sacrificed to idols and from blood and from what is strangled and from fornication." [26]Then Paul took the men, and the next day, having purified himself, he entered the temple with them, making public the completion of the days of purification when the sacrifice would be made for each of them.

Reflection

Another eventful reading comes our way. Here we read the details of Paul's journey to Jerusalem. For our purposes, what is perhaps most notable is that Paul is warned again not to go to Jerusalem. In a very dramatic moment, a prophet "took Paul's belt, bound his own feet and hands with it, and said, 'Thus says the Holy Spirit, "This is the way the Jews in Jerusalem will bind the man who owns this belt and will hand him over to the Gentiles."'" Paul is bold in his desire to follow God's call, saying, "I am ready not only to be bound but even to die in Jerusalem for the name of the Lord Jesus."

Paul is sensible. He knows the danger, but he also knows that God has called him to do a very specific thing. I wonder how different our church would be if we listened carefully, discerning God's will for us, and then pursuing that call relentlessly. Maybe we would do well to focus more on discernment than sensibility. I know that in my own life, I have never regretted answering God's call, once I was clear what I was hearing.

We end with another key episode in the most important pivot of the Book of Acts: The church gradually becomes more open to the Gentiles and more eager to share the good news of Jesus Christ with the whole world, not just the Jews. It's hard to overstate the importance or the radical nature of this shift. In no way do they neglect costly discipleship, but they do find ways to share the gospel with others.

The Rev. Canon Scott Gunn
Executive Director, Forward Movement
Cincinnati, Ohio

Questions

Do you believe that God equips the people whom God calls? Have you experienced this?

Paul is willing to be a Jew for the Jews and a Gentile for the Gentiles, all for the sake of the gospel. What parts of his message never change? What is changeable?

Prayer

Come Holy Spirit, come. Fill our minds with your wisdom, fill our hearts with your courage, fill our mouths with your praise. Then inspire us to do your will. Through Jesus Christ our Lord. *Amen.*

Acts 21:27—22:29

²⁷When the seven days were almost completed, the Jews from Asia, who had seen him in the temple, stirred up the whole crowd. They seized him, ²⁸shouting, "Fellow Israelites, help! This is the man who is teaching everyone everywhere against our people, our law, and this place; more than that, he has actually brought Greeks into the temple and has defiled this holy place." ²⁹For they had previously seen Trophimus the Ephesian with him in the city, and they supposed that Paul had brought him into the temple. ³⁰Then all the city was aroused, and the people rushed together. They seized Paul and dragged him out of the temple, and immediately the doors were shut. ³¹While they were trying to kill him, word came to the tribune of the cohort that all Jerusalem was in an uproar. ³²Immediately he took soldiers and centurions and ran down to them. When they saw the tribune and the soldiers, they stopped beating Paul. ³³Then the tribune came, arrested him, and ordered him to be bound with two chains; he inquired who he was and what he had done. ³⁴Some in the crowd shouted one thing, some another; and as he could not learn the facts because of the uproar, he ordered him to be brought into the barracks. ³⁵When Paul came to the steps, the violence of the mob was so great that he had to be carried by the soldiers. ³⁶The crowd that followed kept shouting, "Away with him!"

³⁷Just as Paul was about to be brought into the barracks, he said to the tribune, "May I say something to you?" The tribune replied, "Do you know Greek? ³⁸Then you are not the Egyptian who recently stirred up a revolt and led the four thousand

assassins out into the wilderness?" ³⁹Paul replied, "I am a Jew, from Tarsus in Cilicia, a citizen of an important city; I beg you, let me speak to the people." ⁴⁰When he had given him permission, Paul stood on the steps and motioned to the people for silence; and when there was a great hush, he addressed them in the Hebrew language, saying:

22 "Brothers and fathers, listen to the defense that I now make before you."

²When they heard him addressing them in Hebrew, they became even more quiet. Then he said:

³"I am a Jew, born in Tarsus in Cilicia, but brought up in this city at the feet of Gamaliel, educated strictly according to our ancestral law, being zealous for God, just as all of you are today. ⁴I persecuted this Way up to the point of death by binding both men and women and putting them in prison, ⁵as the high priest and the whole council of elders can testify about me. From them I also received letters to the brothers in Damascus, and I went there in order to bind those who were there and to bring them back to Jerusalem for punishment.

⁶"While I was on my way and approaching Damascus, about noon a great light from heaven suddenly shone about me. ⁷I fell to the ground and heard a voice saying to me, 'Saul, Saul, why are you persecuting me?' ⁸I answered, 'Who are you, Lord?' Then he said to me, 'I am Jesus of Nazareth whom you are persecuting.' ⁹Now those who were with me saw the light but did not hear the voice of the one who was speaking to me. ¹⁰I asked, 'What am I to do, Lord?' The Lord said to me, 'Get up and go to Damascus; there you will be told everything that has been assigned to you to do.' ¹¹Since I could not see because of the brightness of that light, those who were with me took my hand and led me to Damascus.

12"A certain Ananias, who was a devout man according to the law and well spoken of by all the Jews living there, 13came to me; and standing beside me, he said, 'Brother Saul, regain your sight!' In that very hour I regained my sight and saw him. 14Then he said, 'The God of our ancestors has chosen you to know his will, to see the Righteous One and to hear his own voice; 15for you will be his witness to all the world of what you have seen and heard. 16And now why do you delay? Get up, be baptized, and have your sins washed away, calling on his name.'

17"After I had returned to Jerusalem and while I was praying in the temple, I fell into a trance 18and saw Jesus saying to me, 'Hurry and get out of Jerusalem quickly, because they will not accept your testimony about me.' 19And I said, 'Lord, they themselves know that in every synagogue I imprisoned and beat those who believed in you. 20And while the blood of your witness Stephen was shed, I myself was standing by, approving and keeping the coats of those who killed him.' 21Then he said to me, 'Go, for I will send you far away to the Gentiles.'"

22Up to this point they listened to him, but then they shouted, "Away with such a fellow from the earth! For he should not be allowed to live." 23And while they were shouting, throwing off their cloaks, and tossing dust into the air, 24the tribune directed that he was to be brought into the barracks, and ordered him to be examined by flogging, to find out the reason for this outcry against him. 25But when they had tied him up with thongs, Paul said to the centurion who was standing by, "Is it legal for you to flog a Roman citizen who is uncondemned?" 26When the centurion heard that, he went to the tribune and said to him, "What are you about to do? This man is a Roman citizen." 27The tribune came and asked Paul, "Tell me, are you a Roman citizen?" And he said, "Yes." [28]The tribune answered, "It cost me a large sum of money to get my citizenship." Paul said, "But I was born a citizen." [29]Immediately those who were about to examine him drew back from him; and the tribune also was afraid, for he realized that Paul was a Roman citizen and that he had bound him.

Reflection

The fervor to kill Paul was once again at a fever pitch. While the tribune and soldiers were confused about why so many were so angry at this man, one reason seems clear: He brought outsiders into the temple. He defiled the holy place by inviting unholy people into it.

Even Paul's story of conversion on the Damascus Road didn't set the crowds into an uproar. The frenzy erupted as he finished and recalled Jesus urging him, "Go, for I will send you far away to the Gentiles." Paul's sin? He drew the circle too wide, and suggested that's what God wants all of us to do.

No doubt, the gospel of Jesus Christ is a scandal and a mystery. While most human communities draw clear boundaries and pull their members inside, followers of Jesus are constantly being thrust across dividing lines. It's not as if we like it. Notice how often Christians are the very groups proclaiming who is to be welcomed and who is to be shunned, where a holy person should stand and where a holy person dare not walk. It's the most human instinct to create smaller, safer circles within which to move and believe.

Paul's encounter with Jesus was so stunning it wiped away this way of seeing and being—the way of strict segregation and purity—and replaced it with the light and freedom of Christ. Two thousand years later, the world isn't much more excited about this scandalous way. Thank God that Jesus continues to meet us and draw us over the line, just the same.

The Rev. Canon Stephanie Spellers
The Presiding Bishop's Canon for Evangelism and Reconciliation
New York, New York

Questions

Can you recall a moment in scripture when Jesus crossed a religious boundary or declared holy what others said was impure?

Can you recall a moment when you have been inspired to do the same, in his name?

Prayer

God of Creation, you have made all things in love, and nothing that has breath is alien to you. Grant that we may see the world as you do, and give us grace to behold and receive every person as a child of God, for the sake of your love. *Amen.*

Acts 22:30—23:11

³⁰Since [the tribune] wanted to find out what Paul was being accused of by the Jews, the next day he released him and ordered the chief priests and the entire council to meet. He brought Paul down and had him stand before them.

23 While Paul was looking intently at the council he said, "Brothers, up to this day I have lived my life with a clear conscience before God." ²Then the high priest Ananias ordered those standing near him to strike him on the mouth. ³At this Paul said to him, "God will strike you, you whitewashed wall! Are you sitting there to judge me according to the law, and yet in violation of the law you order me to be struck?" ⁴Those standing nearby said, "Do you dare to insult God's high priest?" ⁵And Paul said, "I did not realize, brothers, that he was high priest; for it is written, 'You shall not speak evil of a leader of your people.'"

⁶When Paul noticed that some were Sadducees and others were Pharisees, he called out in the council, "Brothers, I am a Pharisee, a son of Pharisees. I am on trial concerning the hope of the resurrection of the dead." ⁷When he said this, a dissension began between the Pharisees and the Sadducees, and the assembly was divided. ⁸(The Sadducees say that there is no resurrection, or angel, or spirit; but the Pharisees acknowledge all three.) ⁹Then a great clamor arose, and certain scribes of the Pharisees' group stood up and contended, "We find nothing wrong with this man. What if a spirit or an angel has spoken to him?" ¹⁰When the dissension became violent, the tribune, fearing that they would tear Paul to pieces, ordered the

soldiers to go down, take him by force, and bring him into the barracks.

¹¹That night the Lord stood near him and said, "Keep up your courage! For just as you have testified for me in Jerusalem, so you must bear witness also in Rome."

Reflection

It is a familiar sight: the Apostle Paul deftly parrying in the ring, exposing his accusers' vulnerabilities, sending them into confusion while he lives to witness another day. In so many ways, Paul here fulfills what Jesus promised in Matthew 10:16-20:

> See, I am sending you out like sheep into the midst of wolves; so be wise as serpents and innocent as doves. Beware of them, for they will hand you over to councils and flog you in their synagogues; and you will be dragged before governors and kings because of me…When they hand you over, do not worry about how you are to speak or what you are to say;…for it is not you who speak, but the Spirit of your Father speaking through you.

Paul needs that Spirit like he never has before. Remember that the Sanhedrin were the ruling council of the Jewish people. Once Paul had been their envoy, sent to torture followers of Jesus on the council's behalf. Now he stands before them, an ambassador of Christ. You can almost see the rivulets of sweat running down his face. You can imagine him wracking his brain, like a runaway slave at the crossroads, trying to make a way out of no way.

Paul must have been tempted to rely on his own considerable wit, but maybe Jesus' words rang in his head: "Paul, stop worrying and crafting. I called you to be my witness. Paul, I've got this." The rest flowed.

It's unlikely any of us will face a council quite as fierce as the Sanhedrin. What a relief to know that the Spirit who gave Paul the words, strategy, and grace he so desperately needed is the same Spirit that animates us as Jesus' followers today. Keep up your courage. The Spirit is near.

The Rev. Canon Stephanie Spellers
The Presiding Bishop's Canon for Evangelism and Reconciliation
New York, New York

A Journey Through Acts

Questions_____

Have you ever found yourself at a loss—unsure what to say or do—and experienced God "making a way"? Recall the story.

How did you recognize the presence of God at that time?

Prayer _____

Almighty and ever-present God, our greatest joy is to answer your call and serve your will. Help us to humbly receive the gifts you offer without fail, and to trust that your power working in us is the only power we need. *Amen.*

Acts 23:12-35

¹²In the morning the Jews joined in a conspiracy and bound themselves by an oath neither to eat nor drink until they had killed Paul. ¹³There were more than forty who joined in this conspiracy. ¹⁴They went to the chief priests and elders and said, "We have strictly bound ourselves by an oath to taste no food until we have killed Paul. ¹⁵Now then, you and the council must notify the tribune to bring him down to you, on the pretext that you want to make a more thorough examination of his case. And we are ready to do away with him before he arrives."

¹⁶Now the son of Paul's sister heard about the ambush; so he went and gained entrance to the barracks and told Paul. ¹⁷Paul called one of the centurions and said, "Take this young man to the tribune, for he has something to report to him." ¹⁸So he took him, brought him to the tribune, and said, "The prisoner Paul called me and asked me to bring this young man to you; he has something to tell you." ¹⁹The tribune took him by the hand, drew him aside privately, and asked, "What is it that you have to report to me?" ²⁰He answered, "The Jews have agreed to ask you to bring Paul down to the council tomorrow, as though they were going to inquire more thoroughly into his case. ²¹But do not be persuaded by them, for more than forty of their men are lying in ambush for him. They have bound themselves by an oath neither to eat nor drink until they kill him. They are ready now and are waiting for your consent." ²²So the tribune dismissed the young man, ordering him, "Tell no one that you have informed me of this."

23Then he summoned two of the centurions and said, "Get ready to leave by nine o'clock tonight for Caesarea with two hundred soldiers, seventy horsemen, and two hundred spearmen. 24Also provide mounts for Paul to ride, and take him safely to Felix the governor." 25He wrote a letter to this effect:

26"Claudius Lysias to his Excellency the governor Felix, greetings. 27This man was seized by the Jews and was about to be killed by them, but when I had learned that he was a Roman citizen, I came with the guard and rescued him. 28Since I wanted to know the charge for which they accused him, I had him brought to their council. 29I found that he was accused concerning questions of their law, but was charged with nothing deserving death or imprisonment. 30When I was informed that there would be a plot against the man, I sent him to you at once, ordering his accusers also to state before you what they have against him." 31So the soldiers, according to their instructions, took Paul and brought him during the night to Antipatris. 32The next day they let the horsemen go on with him, while they returned to the barracks. 33When they came to Caesarea and delivered the letter to the governor, they presented Paul also before him. 34On reading the letter, he asked what province he belonged to, and when he learned that he was from Cilicia, 35he said, "I will give you a hearing when your accusers arrive." Then he ordered that he be kept under guard in Herod's headquarters.

Reflection

We press on today with Paul in his difficult encounters with religious and secular authorities, and Saint Luke provides extensive details in this case, describing a plot to kill Paul. Of course, he has been terribly mistreated and hasn't seen the end by far; more suffering, and finally martyrdom, will be his fate, foreshadowed by Jesus' remarkable midnight encouragement reported at Acts 23:11: "You must bear witness also in Rome"—"witness," that is, *martyresai* in Greek.

First Paul finds a reprieve, however, in the form of justice and due process, thanks to the intervention of the Roman tribune in Jerusalem, Claudius Lysias. His decision to sidestep the plot and send Paul to Felix, the Roman governor of Judea, is both creative and fair-minded. True, a critical condition of Paul's protection remains his Roman citizenship, which should cause us to reflect on the universal claim to a fair trial that all human beings are due, irrespective of birth or nationality.

Even so, Paul's vulnerability to the powers of the day—and the image of Claudius Lysias writing to Felix about internal controversies among the Jews—recalls the handling of our Lord on the doorstep of his Passion, passed from Pontius Pilate to Herod and back again (see Luke 23). Luke's depiction here in Acts of Paul's identical treatment powerfully consolidates the truth that Paul has indeed testified for Jesus in Jerusalem (Acts 23:11) just as Jesus himself testified there. What an amazing privilege for Paul to suffer like Jesus, for Jesus, with Jesus. In this way, Paul is paradoxically strengthened by a communion with Christ that is utterly concrete and real, like all true communion.

Dr. Christopher Wells
Executive Director and Editor, The Living Church Foundation
Milwaukee, Wisconsin

Questions_____

Personal questions to ask ourselves before God: How can I bear sacrificial witness to Christ, either in dramatic or seemingly small ways—in my work, relationships, and immediate environment?

How might an acceptance of powerlessness permit God to use me more powerfully as his instrument?

Prayer _____

O Lord God, you go before me in the person of your Son, and teach me to take up my cross and follow: So form me in his likeness, upheld by his prayer, that I may face all adversity with confidence and courage, to the glory of your name. *Amen.*

Acts 24:1-27

24 Five days later the high priest Ananias came down with some elders and an attorney, a certain Tertullus, and they reported their case against Paul to the governor. 2When Paul had been summoned, Tertullus began to accuse him, saying:

"Your Excellency, because of you we have long enjoyed peace, and reforms have been made for this people because of your foresight. 3We welcome this in every way and everywhere with utmost gratitude. 4But, to detain you no further, I beg you to hear us briefly with your customary graciousness. 5We have, in fact, found this man a pestilent fellow, an agitator among all the Jews throughout the world, and a ringleader of the sect of the Nazarenes. 6He even tried to profane the temple, and so we seized him. 8By examining him yourself you will be able to learn from him concerning everything of which we accuse him." 9The Jews also joined in the charge by asserting that all this was true.

10When the governor motioned to him to speak, Paul replied:

"I cheerfully make my defense, knowing that for many years you have been a judge over this nation. 11As you can find out, it is not more than twelve days since I went up to worship in Jerusalem. 12They did not find me disputing with anyone in the temple or stirring up a crowd either in the synagogues or throughout the city. 13Neither can they prove to you the charge that they now bring against me. 14But this I admit to you, that according to the Way, which they call a sect, I worship the God of our ancestors, believing everything laid down according to the law or written in the prophets. 15I have a hope in God—a hope that they themselves also accept—that there will be a resurrection of both the righteous and the unrighteous. [16]Therefore I do my best always to have a clear conscience toward God and all people. [17]Now after some years I came to bring alms to my nation and to offer sacrifices. [18]While I was doing this, they found me in the temple, completing the rite of purification, without any crowd or disturbance. [19]But there were some Jews from Asia—they ought to be here before you to make an accusation, if they have anything against me. [20]Or let these men here tell what crime they had found when I stood before the council, [21]unless it was this one sentence that I called out while standing before them, 'It is about the resurrection of the dead that I am on trial before you today.'"

[22]But Felix, who was rather well informed about the Way, adjourned the hearing with the comment, "When Lysias the tribune comes down, I will decide your case." [23]Then he ordered the centurion to keep him in custody, but to let him have some liberty and not to prevent any of his friends from taking care of his needs.

[24]Some days later when Felix came with his wife Drusilla, who was Jewish, he sent for Paul and heard him speak concerning faith in Christ Jesus. [25]And as he discussed justice, self-control, and the coming judgment, Felix became frightened and said, "Go away for the present; when I have an opportunity, I will send for you." [26]At the same time he hoped that money would be given him by Paul, and for that reason he used to send for him very often and converse with him.

[27]After two years had passed, Felix was succeeded by Porcius Festus; and since he wanted to grant the Jews a favor, Felix left Paul in prison.

Reflection

Saint Luke's vivid evocation of Jewish life under Roman rule presents real challenges both for Paul and for the high priest Ananias and his acolytes. The chapter opens with the lawyer Tertullus walking a tricky tightrope of flattery of the governor and focused indictment of Paul as a putative troublemaker with rebellious tendencies. Paul, in turn, flatly denies causing any disturbance; his interests are theological: "I have a hope in God" (v. 15).

Recall here Paul's famous teaching in Romans 13 that all should "be subject to the governing authorities" as "instituted by God" (13:1). To have said this hardly settles every question of when disobedience may be justified. It does, however, establish a basic principle for a Christian thinking about government, namely, that God establishes and uses secular authorities to achieve justice and maintain order; anarchy is neither desirable nor practicable, for the good reason that "all, both Jews and Greeks, are under the power of sin" (Rom. 3:9).

This being so, Paul models in Acts 24 the peculiar vocation of—again—witness to the truth of God as a gift for *all* the world and not only the religious, whether Jews or followers of the newfound Way. Paul proves himself an evangelist. He speaks clearly and forthrightly, assuming that divine truths, including those concerning "justice, self-control, and the coming judgment" (v. 25), will be of interest to Felix. And he does so "cheerfully" (v. 10), a wonderful word that evokes the spirit of Christian obedience, day by day (see "Collect for the Renewal of Life," *The Book of Common Prayer*, p. 99). When we are cheerful we are "compassionate" (Romans 12:8), enabled to love even our enemies.

Dr. Christopher Wells
Executive Director and Editor, The Living Church Foundation
Milwaukee, Wisconsin

Questions _____

More personal questions: How can I subject myself to authority in a way that helps the powerful to hear and learn God's truth?

How might my cheerfulness garner otherwise unavailable audiences?

Prayer _____

Almighty God, you have made us marvelously in your image, and said that every part of creation is good: Give us the grace to share your gospel with all whom we meet, in the confidence that your word is true and will bear fruit, by the power of your Spirit. *Amen.*

Acts 25:1-22

25 Three days after Festus had arrived in the province, he went up from Caesarea to Jerusalem ²where the chief priests and the leaders of the Jews gave him a report against Paul. They appealed to him ³and requested, as a favor to them against Paul, to have him transferred to Jerusalem. They were, in fact, planning an ambush to kill him along the way. ⁴Festus replied that Paul was being kept at Caesarea, and that he himself intended to go there shortly. ⁵"So," he said, "let those of you who have the authority come down with me, and if there is anything wrong about the man, let them accuse him."

⁶After he had stayed among them not more than eight or ten days, he went down to Caesarea; the next day he took his seat on the tribunal and ordered Paul to be brought. ⁷When he arrived, the Jews who had gone down from Jerusalem surrounded him, bringing many serious charges against him, which they could not prove. ⁸Paul said in his defense, "I have in no way committed an offense against the law of the Jews, or against the temple, or against the emperor." ⁹But Festus, wishing to do the Jews a favor, asked Paul, "Do you wish to go up to Jerusalem and be tried there before me on these charges?" ¹⁰Paul said, "I am appealing to the emperor's tribunal; this is where I should be tried. I have done no wrong to the Jews, as you very well know. ¹¹Now if I am in the wrong and have committed something for which I deserve to die, I am not trying to escape death; but if there is nothing to their charges against me, no one can turn me over to them. I appeal to the emperor." ¹²Then Festus, after he

had conferred with his council, replied, "You have appealed to the emperor; to the emperor you will go."

¹³After several days had passed, King Agrippa and Bernice arrived at Caesarea to welcome Festus. ¹⁴Since they were staying there several days, Festus laid Paul's case before the king, saying, "There is a man here who was left in prison by Felix. ¹⁵When I was in Jerusalem, the chief priests and the elders of the Jews informed me about him and asked for a sentence against him. ¹⁶I told them that it was not the custom of the Romans to hand over anyone before the accused had met the accusers face to face and had been given an opportunity to make a defense against the charge. ¹⁷So when they met here, I lost no time, but on the next day took my seat on the tribunal and ordered the man to be brought. ¹⁸When the accusers stood up, they did not charge him with any of the crimes that I was expecting. ¹⁹Instead they had certain points of disagreement with him about their own religion and about a certain Jesus, who had died, but whom Paul asserted to be alive. ²⁰Since I was at a loss how to investigate these questions, I asked whether he wished to go to Jerusalem and be tried there on these charges. ²¹But when Paul had appealed to be kept in custody for the decision of his Imperial Majesty, I ordered him to be held until I could send him to the emperor." ²²Agrippa said to Festus, "I would like to hear the man myself." "Tomorrow," he said, "you will hear him."

Reflection

I have a friend who has had a form of synesthesia since childhood. He claimed that every number was clearly associated with a color. There were correlations and relationships in his mind that made no sense to me at all. I wonder if Festus felt a similar confusion when Paul came before him in Caesarea.

In navigating the Roman legal system, Paul must have looked savvy. Claiming his right as a citizen to trial by the emperor would have made sense to Festus. Paul was just trying to save his own skin. But the particulars of the case were strange. The dispute was religious. It was about whether an executed Jew was somehow still alive. Even if the ridiculous proposition were true, why would it matter? It must have sounded like arguing about the color of the number seven to poor Festus. But for some reason, Festus stayed curious. Sometimes meeting a person whose whole way of seeing is different from yours is compelling, not alienating.

Paul seems to relish and thrive in these places of misunderstanding between cultures and worldviews. Remember him in Athens a few chapters back, using the idol to the unknown god as a way in to the gospel?

So often I want my life to make sense to the people I encounter. I want to find points of intersection and commonality, and downplay difference. But Paul's story suggests that moments of incomprehension can be rich with possibility, especially when I risk telling how the resurrected Christ has radically altered the way I see the world.

The Rev. Scott Walters
Rector, Calvary Episcopal Church
Memphis, Tennessee

A Journey Through Acts

Question _____

Think back on a time or two in your life when you had the strength to tell a deep truth about yourself or your faith, strange as it must have sounded to your hearers. What happened in the relationship after you were vulnerable in this way?

How did it affect your relationship with God and your knowledge of yourself?

Prayer _____

God of grace, too often we look for love and affirmation first from other human beings rather than you; strengthen our trust in the redeeming love of the risen Christ, that we may bear clearer witness to the hope that is in us, that others may come to the liberating knowledge of your love; through Jesus Christ our Lord. *Amen.*

Acts 25:23—26:32

²³So on the next day Agrippa and Bernice came with great pomp, and they entered the audience hall with the military tribunes and the prominent men of the city. Then Festus gave the order and Paul was brought in. ²⁴And Festus said, "King Agrippa and all here present with us, you see this man about whom the whole Jewish community petitioned me, both in Jerusalem and here, shouting that he ought not to live any longer. ²⁵But I found that he had done nothing deserving death; and when he appealed to his Imperial Majesty, I decided to send him. ²⁶But I have nothing definite to write to our sovereign about him. Therefore I have brought him before all of you, and especially before you, King Agrippa, so that, after we have examined him, I may have something to write—²⁷for it seems to me unreasonable to send a prisoner without indicating the charges against him."

26 Agrippa said to Paul, "You have permission to speak for yourself." Then Paul stretched out his hand and began to defend himself: ²

"I consider myself fortunate that it is before you, King Agrippa, I am to make my defense today against all the accusations of the Jews, ³because you are especially familiar with all the customs and controversies of the Jews; therefore I beg of you to listen to me patiently.

⁴"All the Jews know my way of life from my youth, a life spent from the beginning among my own people and in Jerusalem. ⁵They have known for a long time, if they are willing to testify, that I have belonged to the strictest sect of our religion and

lived as a Pharisee. 6And now I stand here on trial on account of my hope in the promise made by God to our ancestors, 7a promise that our twelve tribes hope to attain, as they earnestly worship day and night. It is for this hope, your Excellency, that I am accused by Jews! 8Why is it thought incredible by any of you that God raises the dead?

9"Indeed, I myself was convinced that I ought to do many things against the name of Jesus of Nazareth. 10And that is what I did in Jerusalem; with authority received from the chief priests, I not only locked up many of the saints in prison, but I also cast my vote against them when they were being condemned to death. 11By punishing them often in all the synagogues I tried to force them to blaspheme; and since I was so furiously enraged at them, I pursued them even to foreign cities.

12"With this in mind, I was traveling to Damascus with the authority and commission of the chief priests, 13when at midday along the road, your Excellency, I saw a light from heaven, brighter than the sun, shining around me and my companions. 14When we had all fallen to the ground, I heard a voice saying to me in the Hebrew language, 'Saul, Saul, why are you persecuting me? It hurts you to kick against the goads.' 15I asked, 'Who are you, Lord?' The Lord answered, 'I am Jesus whom you are persecuting. 16But get up and stand on your feet; for I have appeared to you for this purpose, to appoint you to serve and testify to the things in which you have seen me and to those in which I will appear to you. 17I will rescue you from your people and from the Gentiles— to whom I am sending you 18to open their eyes so that they may turn from darkness to light and from the power of Satan to God, so that they may receive forgiveness of sins and a place among those who are sanctified by faith in me.'

¹⁹"After that, King Agrippa, I was not disobedient to the heavenly vision, ²⁰but declared first to those in Damascus, then in Jerusalem and throughout the countryside of Judea, and also to the Gentiles, that they should repent and turn to God and do deeds consistent with repentance. ²¹For this reason the Jews seized me in the temple and tried to kill me. ²²To this day I have had help from God, and so I stand here, testifying to both small and great, saying nothing but what the prophets and Moses said would take place: ²³that the Messiah must suffer, and that, by being the first to rise from the dead, he would proclaim light both to our people and to the Gentiles."

²⁴While he was making this defense, Festus exclaimed, "You are out of your mind, Paul! Too much learning is driving you insane!" ²⁵But Paul said, "I am not out of your mind, most excellent Festus, but I am speaking the sober truth. ²⁶Indeed the king knows about these things, and to him I speak freely; for I am certain that none of these things has escaped his notice, for this was not done in a corner. ²⁷King Agrippa, do you believe the prophets? I know that you believe." ²⁸Agrippa said to Paul, "Are you so quickly persuading me to become a Christian?" ²⁹Paul replied, "Whether quickly or not, I pray to God that not only you but also all who are listening to me today might become such as I am—except for these chains."

³⁰Then the king got up, and with him the governor and Bernice and those who had been seated with them; ³¹and as they were leaving, they said to one another, "This man is doing nothing to deserve death or imprisonment." ³²Agrippa said to Festus, "This man could have been set free if he had not appealed to the emperor."

Reflection

Countless plotlines hang on a bad guy getting what's coming to him. There are conversion stories, too, in the books and movies we love. But if we're honest, even in the most famous conversion of them all, a Spaghetti Western sort of satisfaction can arise in a reader when smug old Saul (who lived to tell and became Paul) gets knocked off his high horse and lectured by Jesus from the sky. Surely his humiliation helps bring the moral universe a little more into balance.

The human satisfaction in revenge is instinctive, but deeply counter to the gospel of grace. And maybe it's why we miss the grace in Jesus' words to Saul as he's lying on the Damascus road. "Saul…It hurts you to kick against the goads." Even after the resurrection, with a voice that booms from the sky in a flash of light, Jesus' concern is not for his own wounds, but for those of his persecutor.

How about that? The resurrected savior is not some righteous conqueror who avenges the world's wrongs one by one. That's a pretty good description of the unconverted Saul. The risen Christ is Jesus: the one who told us never to return evil for evil, to turn our cheek rather than striking back, to return blessings whenever we're cursed. The one whose message even to the enemy lying flat on his back on the road was, "Your vengeful kicks hurt only yourself, Saul. I'm going to free you from this pain."

The Rev. Scott Walters
Rector, Calvary Episcopal Church
Memphis, Tennessee

Question _____

Bring to mind a moment when you realized that anger, perhaps even at some real injustice, was hurting you and not making the world better. How did God bring you to this realization?

What did getting free from the grip of vengeance feel like?

Prayer _____

Forgiving God, who is always more ready to give mercy than we are to receive it, heal us of our self-destructive ways, especially our vengeance, our anger, our righteous indignation, that we might know the freedom for which we were created; in the name of the risen and merciful Christ. *Amen.*

Acts 27:1-12

27 When it was decided that we were to sail for Italy, they transferred Paul and some other prisoners to a centurion of the Augustan Cohort, named Julius. ²Embarking on a ship of Adramyttium that was about to set sail to the ports along the coast of Asia, we put to sea, accompanied by Aristarchus, a Macedonian from Thessalonica. ³The next day we put in at Sidon; and Julius treated Paul kindly, and allowed him to go to his friends to be cared for. ⁴Putting out to sea from there, we sailed under the lee of Cyprus, because the winds were against us. ⁵After we had sailed across the sea that is off Cilicia and Pamphylia, we came to Myra in Lycia. ⁶There the centurion found an Alexandrian ship bound for Italy and put us on board. ⁷We sailed slowly for a number of days and arrived with difficulty off Cnidus, and as the wind was against us, we sailed under the lee of Crete off Salmone. ⁸Sailing past it with difficulty, we came to a place called Fair Havens, near the city of Lasea.

9 Since much time had been lost and sailing was now dangerous, because even the Fast had already gone by, Paul advised them, ¹⁰saying, "Sirs, I can see that the voyage will be with danger and much heavy loss, not only of the cargo and the ship, but also of our lives." ¹¹But the centurion paid more attention to the pilot and to the owner of the ship than to what Paul said. ¹²Since the harbor was not suitable for spending the winter, the majority was in favor of putting to sea from there, on the chance that somehow they could reach Phoenix, where they could spend the winter. It was a harbor of Crete, facing southwest and northwest.

Reflection

Having appealed to Caesar, as was his right as a Roman citizen, Paul begins what was to be his last and rather eventful journey to Rome. The apostle, who had in his letters called himself "a slave for Jesus' sake" finds himself literally enslaved, in the sense that he is not free to do as he pleases, but is a prisoner of the Roman State. He has to defend himself against the charge of undermining the Jewish faith, thereby creating unrest in his preaching of the gospel of Jesus. This was not the way he had intended to come to Rome, the capital city of the Empire. He had written a letter to the Christian community already established there and had always hoped to come in person to expound upon what he had written. He now finds himself coming under very different circumstances, but in spite of that decides to use it as an opportunity to spread the gospel. Paul, who had already suffered much in proclaiming the Lordship of Christ, always used whatever circumstance he faced as a means of furthering his mission. Every event and occasion became a means of spreading the news about Jesus. Paul never gives up when life is less than favorable. Adversity seems just to strengthen his resolve as he "presses on towards the goal," as he writes elsewhere.

As was his usual custom Paul travels with companions—Aristarchus and an unnamed narrator. Paul realized the gospel was more credible when it had more than one advocate and he always entrusted leadership of the churches he founded to a group of elders, not just one. "It takes a community to manifest the grace present in Jesus," offers one commentator.

The Rt. Rev. Dr. Barry C. Morgan
Archbishop of Wales and Bishop of Llandaff
Cardiff, Wales

A Journey Through Acts

Questions _____

Can you think of unfavorable events in you have used to bear witness to the gospel?

How easy do you find it to work alongside others?

Prayer _____

Almighty God, help us to see that whatever situation we face can be used to further your purposes. Give us insight to see opportunities where others see only threats, and enable us to appreciate the gifts others may bring to all that confronts us. *Amen.*

Acts 27:13—28:31

¹³When a moderate south wind began to blow, they thought they could achieve their purpose; so they weighed anchor and began to sail past Crete, close to the shore. ¹⁴But soon a violent wind, called the northeaster, rushed down from Crete. ¹⁵Since the ship was caught and could not be turned head-on into the wind, we gave way to it and were driven. ¹⁶By running under the lee of a small island called Cauda we were scarcely able to get the ship's boat under control. ¹⁷After hoisting it up they took measures to undergird the ship; then, fearing that they would run on the Syrtis, they lowered the sea anchor and so were driven. ¹⁸We were being pounded by the storm so violently that on the next day they began to throw the cargo overboard, ¹⁹and on the third day with their own hands they threw the ship's tackle overboard.

²⁰When neither sun nor stars appeared for many days, and no small tempest raged, all hope of our being saved was at last abandoned.

²¹Since they had been without food for a long time, Paul then stood up among them and said, "Men, you should have listened to me and not have set sail from Crete and thereby avoided this damage and loss. ²²I urge you now to keep up your courage, for there will be no loss of life among you, but only of the ship. ²³For last night there stood by me an angel of the God to whom I belong and whom I worship, ²⁴and he said, 'Do not be afraid, Paul; you must stand before the emperor; and indeed, God has granted safety to all those who are sailing with you.' ²⁵So keep up your courage, men, for I have faith in God that it will be exactly as I have been told. ²⁶But

we will have to run aground on some island."

27When the fourteenth night had come, as we were drifting across the sea of Adria, about midnight the sailors suspected that they were nearing land. 28So they took soundings and found twenty fathoms; a little farther on they took soundings again and found fifteen fathoms. 29Fearing that we might run on the rocks, they let down four anchors from the stern and prayed for day to come. 30But when the sailors tried to escape from the ship and had lowered the boat into the sea, on the pretext of putting out anchors from the bow, 31Paul said to the centurion and the soldiers, "Unless these men stay in the ship, you cannot be saved." 32Then the soldiers cut away the ropes of the boat and set it adrift.

33Just before daybreak, Paul urged all of them to take some food, saying, "Today is the fourteenth day that you have been in suspense and remaining without food, having eaten nothing. 34Therefore I urge you to take some food, for it will help you survive; for none of you will lose a hair from your heads."35After he had said this, he took bread; and giving thanks to God in the presence of all, he broke it and began to eat. 36Then all of them were encouraged and took food for themselves. 37(We were in all two hundred seventy-six persons in the ship.) 38After they had satisfied their hunger, they lightened the ship by throwing the wheat into the sea.

39In the morning they did not recognize the land, but they noticed a bay with a beach, on which they planned to run the ship ashore, if they could. 40So they cast off the anchors and left them in the sea. At the same time they loosened the ropes that tied the steering-oars; then hoisting the foresail to the wind, they made for the beach. 41But striking a reef, they ran the ship aground; the bow stuck and remained immovable, but the stern was being broken up by the force of the waves. ⁴²The soldiers' plan was to kill the prisoners, so that none might swim away and escape; ⁴³but the centurion, wishing to save Paul, kept them from carrying out their plan. He ordered those who could swim to jump overboard first and make for the land, ⁴⁴and the rest to follow, some on planks and others on pieces of the ship. And so it was that all were brought safely to land.

28 After we had reached safety, we then learned that the island was called Malta. ²The natives showed us unusual kindness. Since it had begun to rain and was cold, they kindled a fire and welcomed all of us around it. ³Paul had gathered a bundle of brushwood and was putting it on the fire, when a viper, driven out by the heat, fastened itself on his hand. ⁴When the natives saw the creature hanging from his hand, they said to one another, "This man must be a murderer; though he has escaped from the sea, justice has not allowed him to live." ⁵He, however, shook off the creature into the fire and suffered no harm. ⁶They were expecting him to swell up or drop dead, but after they had waited a long time and saw that nothing unusual had happened to him, they changed their minds and began to say that he was a god.

⁷Now in the neighborhood of that place were lands belonging to the leading man of the island, named Publius, who received us and entertained us hospitably for three days. ⁸It so happened that the father of Publius lay sick in bed with fever and dysentery. Paul visited him and cured him by praying and putting his hands on him. ⁹After this happened, the rest of the people on the island who had diseases also came and were cured. ¹⁰They bestowed many honors on us, and when we were about to sail, they put on board all the provisions we needed.

¹¹Three months later we set sail on a ship that had wintered at the island, an Alexandrian

ship with the Twin Brothers as its figurehead. ¹²We put in at Syracuse and stayed there for three days; ¹³then we weighed anchor and came to Rhegium. After one day there a south wind sprang up, and on the second day we came to Puteoli. ¹⁴There we found believers and were invited to stay with them for seven days. And so we came to Rome. ¹⁵The believers from there, when they heard of us, came as far as the Forum of Appius and Three Taverns to meet us. On seeing them, Paul thanked God and took courage.

¹⁶When we came into Rome, Paul was allowed to live by himself, with the soldier who was guarding him.

¹⁷Three days later he called together the local leaders of the Jews. When they had assembled, he said to them, "Brothers, though I had done nothing against our people or the customs of our ancestors, yet I was arrested in Jerusalem and handed over to the Romans.

¹⁸When they had examined me, the Romans wanted to release me, because there was no reason for the death penalty in my case. ¹⁹But when the Jews objected, I was compelled to appeal to the emperor—even though I had no charge to bring against my nation. ²⁰For this reason therefore I have asked to see you and speak with you, since it is for the sake of the hope of Israel that I am bound with this chain." ²¹They replied, "We have received no letters from Judea about you, and none of the brothers coming here has reported or spoken anything evil about you. ²²But we would like to hear from you what you think, for with regard to this sect we know that everywhere it is spoken against."

²³After they had set a day to meet with him, they came to him at his lodgings in great numbers. From morning until evening he explained the matter to them, testifying to the kingdom of God and trying to convince them about Jesus both from the law

of Moses and from the prophets. [24]Some were convinced by what he had said, while others refused to believe. [25]So they disagreed with each other; and as they were leaving, Paul made one further statement: "The Holy Spirit was right in saying to your ancestors through the prophet Isaiah,

[26]'Go to this people and say,
You will indeed listen, but
    never understand,
    and you will indeed look,
        but never perceive.
[27]For this people's heart
    has grown dull,
    and their ears are hard
        of hearing,
    and they have shut their
        eyes;
so that they might not
    look with their eyes,
and listen with their ears,
and understand with
    their heart and
    turn—
and I would heal them.'

[28]Let it be known to you then that this salvation of God has been sent to the Gentiles; they will listen."

[30]He lived there two whole years at his own expense and welcomed all who came to him, [31]proclaiming the kingdom of God and teaching about the Lord Jesus Christ with all boldness and without hindrance.

Reflection

Prisoners tended to be transported to Rome on board grain ships crossing the Mediterranean, and it was on such a ship that Paul was probably boarded. They tended to avoid the open sea, especially in winter, partly because of the weather but partly because Jews regarded the sea as containing the forces of chaos and darkness. Paul's ship however, sailed in winter, against his advice, and shipwreck ensued. He utters the words of Jesus during another storm at sea, "Do not be afraid," and assures the ship's company that they will all be saved. He has faith in the presence of God, who might not be able to save either the ship or its cargo, but who will be with them facing every danger and obstacle. That is the heart of the gospel of Jesus—that God cannot use magic to take away the tragedies and vicissitudes of our lives but does assure us of his love at all times. In the midst of it all Paul also gives thanks to God as the ship's company shares a meal, in words that are reminiscent of Jesus' words at the last supper of taking, blessing, breaking, and sharing bread.

When he eventually arrives in Rome, Paul sets about trying to convince the Jews living there that Jesus is God's Messiah and that in accepting his lordship the need to observe the Jewish law has been superseded. The unconditional love of God proclaimed and embodied in Jesus is to be preached in every place and to the end of time. A sect which began within Judaism is set to become a global faith and religion.

The Rt. Rev. Dr. Barry C. Morgan
Archbishop of Wales and Bishop of Llandaff
Cardiff, Wales

Questions_____

Have there been occasions in your life when God seems to be absent? How easy is it to live by grace and not by rules and regulations?

Prayer _____

Lord God, help us to realize that you are with us especially at times of anguish and distress, for you are a God of compassion, mercy and grace. Help us in turn to live by those values in our dealings with one another. *Amen.*

About the Authors

Dr. Harry W. Attridge is the Sterling Professor of Divinity at the Yale Divinity School in New Haven, Connecticut. He was born in 1946 and educated at Boston College, Cambridge University (as a Marshall Scholar), and Harvard University, where he received his doctorate in 1975. He previously served on the faculties of Perkins School of Theology, Southern Methodist University, and the University of Notre Dame. He has been on the Yale Divinity faculty since 1997 and served as Dean of the school from 2002-2012.

The Rt. Rev. Mariann Edgar Budde gratefully serves as the ninth bishop of the Episcopal Diocese of Washington. She is passionate about congregational life and Christian discipleship. She has dedicated her life to the spiritual renewal and structural transformation of the Episcopal Church so that we might offer the best of who we are to Christ's mission of love in this world.

The Rev. Elizabeth R. Costello serves as associate rector at St. Thomas' Episcopal Church, Whitemarsh, and chaplain to St. Thomas' Nursery School in Fort Washington, Pennsylvania. Outside of work, Liz can be found laughing at the incessant jokes of her husband, the Rev. Joseph G. Wolyniak, chasing after her toddler, Evelyn Thérèse Costello-Wolyniak, or savoring alone time at the gym.

Dr. David Creech is assistant professor of religion at Concordia College in Moorhead, Minnesota. Prior to earning his Ph.D. in theology from Loyola University Chicago, David earned a B.A. in anthropology from the University of California at Santa Barbara and an M.Div. from Fuller Theological Seminary in Pasadena, California. He spends most of his days reading, thinking, teaching, and writing on early Christianities. In his free time he works as a short-order cook for his three delightful kids.

The Very Rev. Albert R. Cutié is a priest in the Episcopal Diocese of Southeast Florida, where he is rector of St. Benedict's Episcopal Church

Church in Plantation, Florida, and presently serves as dean of Broward. He is the author of three books and has had the unique opportunity to juggle his ministry as parish priest with extensive work in various forms of media. He received his Doctor of Ministry degree in Preaching from the University of the South in Sewanee, Tennessee, where he is a member of the Board of Trustees.

THE RT. REV. C. ANDREW DOYLE serves as the ninth bishop of the Episcopal Diocese of Texas and describes his ministry in six words: "Met Jesus on pilgrimage, still walking." Bishop Doyle is most passionate about ministry that takes place outside the walls of the church. He is the author of several books including *A Generous Community: Being the Church in a New Missionary Age* and *Unabashedly Episcopalian: Proclaiming the Good News of the Episcopal Church.* He and his wife JoAnne have two children and live in Houston.

THE REV. CANON SCOTT GUNN is the executive director of Forward Movement, a ministry of the Episcopal Church that inspires disciples and empowers evangelists. Before Forward Movement, he was a parish priest in the Diocese of Rhode Island, and he worked in information technology prior to that. Educated at Luther College (Decorah, Iowa), Yale Divinity School, and Brown University, he lives in Cincinnati with his spouse and somewhat Internet-famous dog.

THE RT. REV. DANIEL G. P. GUTIERREZ is the sixteenth bishop of the extraordinary Episcopal Diocese of Pennsylvania. Throughout his life, he has enjoyed the wondrous experience of "chasing Jesus." He considers himself a (budding and sometimes clumsy but always eager) apprentice of Jesus, most influenced by His words to Peter: "Feed my sheep."

THE REV. MELISSA HOLLERITH and the **VERY REV. RANDOLPH MARSHALL HOLLERITH** have been married for twenty-nine years. Melissa is the former chaplain of St. Christopher's School in Richmond, Virginia. Randy currently serves as the dean of Washington National Cathedral in Washington, D.C.

THE MOST REV. COLIN R. JOHNSON is metropolitan (archbishop) of the Province of Ontario with responsibility for two dioceses: Toronto (one of the largest, most diverse in North America by population) and Moosonee (with a tiny population spread across a huge geography). Ordained for forty years, he served city, rural, and suburban parishes, and on diocesan staff before being elected bishop fourteen years ago. He is a strong advocate for new missional approaches as well as diverse traditional parish ministries to proclaim the gospel of Jesus Christ.

THE VERY REV. JUSTIN ALAN LINDSTROM is the dean of Saint Paul's Episcopal Cathedral in Oklahoma City and the Diocese of Oklahoma. He has a heart for people and a strong desire to share the love of God with all. He is a dynamic communicator, effective teacher, and caring leader.

SANDRA T. MONTES, ED.D. is the Spanish language consultant for the Episcopal Church Foundation. She is a mother, musician, writer, speaker, translator, and educator. She was born in Perú and grew up in Guatemala and el Valle de Texas. Sandra has a doctorate in education and taught for twenty-one years in public elementary schools before becoming a full-time freelance consultant and musician.

THE RT. REV. DR. BARRY C. MORGAN was archbishop of Wales from 2003 to 2017, a post he held in conjunction with being bishop of Llandaff from 1999 to 2017. He was bishop of Bangor from 1993 to 1999 and is currently pro chancellor of the University of Wales and a fellow of the Learned Society of Wales.

BRENDAN O'SULLIVAN-HALE is canon to the ordinary for administration and evangelism in the Episcopal Diocese of Indianapolis. He is a member of the Episcopal Church of All Saints, Indianapolis. Together with Holli Powell, he co-hosts *The Collect Call*, a podcast about *The Book of Common Prayer*.

THE VERY REV. STEVEN A. PEAY is a research professor of homiletics and the former dean-president at Nashotah House Theological Seminary, and honorary canon of Christ Church Cathedral, Eau Claire, Wisconsin. He holds degrees from Greenville College, Saint Vincent Seminary, and the University of Pittsburgh, and received his Ph.D. from Saint Louis University. He is the author of many publications, including articles in *The Encyclopedia of Protestantism* and *Feasting on the Word.*

HOLLI S. POWELL, CPA, is an occasional lay preacher, an amateur photographer, a podcaster (*The Collect Call*, discussing the intersection of life and the Episcopal liturgy), and a member of the Executive Council of the Episcopal Church. In her day job, she serves as the vice president for finance and operations for a nonprofit organization seeking to transform the economy in Appalachia. She lives with her daughter and her two cats in Lexington, Kentucky.

THE REV. SPENCER REECE is the national secretary for Obispo Don Carlos Lopez-Lozano, in the Episcopal Church of Spain, an extra-provincial jurisdiction within the Anglican Communion, reporting directly to the Archbishop of Canterbury. He is the author of *The Clerk's Tale* and *The Road to Emmaus: Poems* and has edited the forthcoming *Counting Time Like People Count Stars*, an anthology of poems by the girls of Our Little Roses, a home for girls in San Pedro Sula, Honduras.

THE VEN. CANON BILL SCHWARTZ, OBE is archdeacon of the Arabian Gulf countries in the Anglican Diocese of Cyprus and the Gulf. He has lived and worked in the Middle East for forty-five years. He holds a Doctor of Ministry degree from Nashotah House Seminary and is the author of *Islam: A Religion, A Culture, A Society.*

THE REV. JAY SIDEBOTHAM serves as director of RenewalWorks, a ministry of Forward Movement that seeks to build cultures of discipleship in Episcopal congregations. Ordained since 1990, he has worked in a number of parishes. He is married to Frances Murchison and resides in Wilmington, North Carolina. He likes to draw cartoons.

EMILY SLICHTER-GIVEN is the director of parish participation at St. Thomas' Episcopal Church, Whitemarsh, in Fort Washington,

Pennsylvania. Her background is in social work, Christian formation, and professional organizing. Emily, a mother of two, is a mixed media artist and author of *Building Faith Brick by Brick: An Imaginative Way to Explore the Bible with Children.*

THE REV. CANON SUSAN BROWN SNOOK is canon for church growth and development in the Episcopal Diocese of Oklahoma and previously served as church planter and rector of the Episcopal Church of the Nativity in Scottsdale, Arizona. She received her Master of Divinity degree from Church Divinity School of the Pacific and is currently working toward a Doctor of Ministry degree from Virginia Theological Seminary. She is the author of *God Gave the Growth: Church Planting in the Episcopal Church.*

THE REV. CANON STEPHANIE SPELLERS serves as the presiding bishop's canon for evangelism and reconciliation, helping Episcopalians to follow Jesus and grow in love for God, our neighbors, and creation. The author of *Radical Welcome: Embracing God, The Other and the Spirit of Transformation* and (with Eric Law) *The Episcopal Way*, she has directed mission and evangelism work at General Theological Seminary and in the Diocese of Long Island; launched The Crossing, a ground-breaking church plant within St. Paul's Cathedral in Boston; and led numerous church-wide renewal efforts.

THE REV. CHAD SUNDIN, OSBC is a Benedictine canon and prior of the Community of St. Mary of the Annunciation, the chaplain for Episcopal Campus Ministries at Arizona State University, and the vicar of St. Augustine's Episcopal Parish in Tempe, Arizona. He is married with three boys, two in high school and one in elementary school. He hangs out with students a lot at his house and in coffee shops, bars, and chapels, and he blogs about the Rule of St. Benedict and its relationship to contemporary life at stmarycanons.org/blog.

THE REV. SCOTT WALTERS is rector of Calvary Episcopal Church in Memphis, Tennessee. Prior to entering Virginia Theological Seminary in

2002, he spent a decade working as a carpenter and house builder in the Pacific Northwest and Arkansas.

Dr. Christopher Wells is executive director and editor of The Living Church Foundation, Inc., based in Milwaukee and Dallas. He oversees the publishing, budget, fundraising, marketing, and staff of *The Living Church*. Christopher completed doctoral studies in historical theology at the University of Notre Dame and teaches when he can at Nashotah House and the General Theological Seminary.

The Rev. Marek P. Zabriskie is the rector of St. Thomas' Episcopal Church, Whitemarsh, in Fort Washington, Pennsylvania, outside of Philadelphia. He founded The Bible Challenge and the Center for Biblical Studies, which promotes and shares The Bible Challenge globally. Since its founding in 2011, The Bible Challenge has had nearly a million people participate. He has edited six books for Forward Movement relating to The Bible Challenge and has written *Doing the Bible Better: The Bible Challenge and the Transformation of the Episcopal Church*. He has also served churches in Nashville, Tennessee, and Richmond, Virginia. To learn more about The Bible Challenge, visit: www.thecenterforbiblicalstudies.org

About Forward Movement

Forward Movement is committed to inspiring disciples and empowering evangelists. We live out our ministry through publishing books, daily reflections, studies for small groups, and online resources. More than a half million people read our daily devotions through *Forward Day by Day*, which is also available in Spanish (*Adelante Día a Día*) and Braille, online, as a podcast, and as an app for your smartphones or tablets. We actively seek partners across the church and look for ways to provide resources that inspire and challenge. A ministry of the Episcopal Church for eighty years, Forward Movement is a nonprofit organization funded by sales of resources and gifts from generous donors. To learn more, visit www.forwardmovement.org.